The
Invisible
Hand
Wielding the Scalpel

The Hidden Cause of America's Healthcare Crisis

Erica Rowe Urquhart, M.D., Ph.D., M.B.A.

Published by:

AUTHORS on **MISSION**

To Mother, with respect and gratitude.

To Marc, with love.

To Amari and Alexis, with inspiration and awe.

Some names and details have been changed for privacy or narrative purposes.

Table of Contents

Introduction

When Claudia Nichols lumbered into our office on crutches, I knew I wanted to help her... and her mother.

Hers was an all too common occurrence.

A young girl with a less-than-desirable insurance plan presented to the emergency room with an ankle fracture that was unstable. She required surgery, open reduction internal fixation, to fully recover from her injury. However, the original on-call team at the hospital where she was taken decided to defer definitive treatment. The ER doctor placed her ankle in a splint, gave her crutches, and instructions. Find a surgeon who participates in her plan.

By the time she and her mother found our private practice, 38 miles away, Claudia was nearing two full weeks after her initial injury, the time when all fractures begin to solidify, whether properly aligned or not.

"Dr. Urquhart, the room is ready. Can we bring your patient back?"

The charge nurse met me at the door of the operating room. She walked through the double doors of Room 7 while I followed.

"Let's get started!" I nudged her with a smile.

I was relieved there would be no delays, but just as I was about to enter the operating room with the patient on the stretcher, I heard someone call my name from the front desk.

The nurse leaned over the counter, scratching her hair cover. Bending her head close to mine and speaking just loud enough for me to hear, she said, "It looks like there's an issue with the next patient's insurance. They're waiting for you in the business office."

What could be wrong? I walked to the door where patient finances were handled, realizing that until now, I had never entered the small room with its spartan desk and two hard chairs. Without preamble, Bryan, the business manager, said, "It's USChoice. The patient's insurer is insisting on a waiting period, even though you and the hospital are in-network. They won't green-light the surgery."

"They what? Oh, they refused to issue the expedited prior authorization. Bryan, please get USChoice on the line. Let me try to get the auth."

He punched the numbers into the phone. "Hello, this is Bryan with the Medical Center calling back regarding patient Claudia Nichols. The surgeon would like to speak with you." He handed me the receiver.

I reached for the telephone, my stomach growling. The mere thought of this conversation had my acid reflux acting up again.

"May I help you?" The man's voice was clipped, detached, and cold.

"Yes, my name is Dr. Erica Rowe Urquhart, and I'd like to review the circumstances of this case. It is an orthopedic urgency because of the prior delay of emergent surgery..."

He interrupted, "The specific circumstances of Miss Nichols' case are irrelevant. USChoice's policy is that this procedure is elective, and the 72-hour waiting period will be enforced... without exception."

It was my turn to interrupt. "Do you mean that an adolescent who presented to an emergency room two weeks ago with an operative fracture has no alternative but to wait another week, until the fracture is almost healed, to have definitive surgical treatment? Just so you know, this is not the orthopedic standard of care."

"That is correct. Not the standard of care part, but the authorization, as the expedited authorization was not granted. The surgery will not be authorized for 72 hours, or three business days. Is there anything else I may help you with?"

I imagined his smug face while I tamped down my outrage and frustration. "We'd like to appeal this decision to your supervisor. The OR is ready, the instruments are sterilized, and the trays have been opened. A significant investment of time and money has already been made by the hospital and our practice to get this young lady to the OR."

"Doctor, our appeals process also requires a 72-hour timeframe for completion. The prior authorization will not be granted today."

"She has to have surgery," I said as if the insurance rep would listen. "Claudia's fracture can't be treated without an operation!"

He ignored my plea. "Have a nice day."

I handed the receiver back to Bryan. "Dr. Urquhart," he asked. "What was the verdict?"

"Bryan, I apologize for the delay. Unfortunately, Claudia Nichols will not be having surgery today. Let me deliver the news to the patient's mother. Can you please call the operating room and ask them to help the patient get changed? She's going home."

I gave Claudia's mother the news, watching her jaw drop, and her shoulders collapse. She swiped at her eyes. "I am so sorry." I reached for her arm, projecting a calm demeanor I did not feel. "Our team did everything we could. USChoice wouldn't authorize Claudia's surgery today. They are strictly enforcing a 72-hour waiting period."

I handed Claudia's mother the doctor's note excusing her absence from work and another letter excusing Claudia's absence from school. She handed Claudia's letter back to me. "Is there something wrong with the letter? Are the dates incorrect?" I asked, wondering if my frustration had caused me to make a mistake.

"No. It's just that Claudia won't be going to school for quite some time. At least not until she can walk without her crutches. The school policy does not allow students to use crutches. They may be a safety hazard or used as a weapon."

Horror stories like this are all too common in the United States healthcare system. Patients like Claudia are the hidden examples of America's healthcare crisis. Too many patients are denied the timely care they need. Sadly, there are reports that as many as 75% of patients abandoned seeking care because of obstacles like Claudia experienced.[1] Deny, Delay, Defer is the insurer's playbook for dealing with patients seeking healthcare. The process of obtaining care is increasingly inefficient. Doctors, nurses, and patients find themselves on hold for days or weeks, waiting for health insurance corporations to decide if a treatment plan is approved or denied. 91% of doctors believe that prior authorization practices negatively impact patients.[2] A breast surgeon was even called out of the operating room as she was about to perform life-saving surgery on a cancer patient. The prior authorization to perform the surgery was revoked during the procedure.

Many insurance companies have become economic predators, denying claims, paying out as little as possible, increasing copays, and dictating what kind of care patients receive. Again, 91% of doctors in an American Medical Association survey reported experiencing delays because of corporate health insurance obstacles. It has taken 20 years in medical practice for me to realize that the American healthcare system is working exactly as it is intended to operate.

---

[1] Yang, E., & Yang, S. (2020). Prior authorization: Overwhelming burden and critical need for reform. *JACC: Case Reports, 2*(10), 1466–1469. https://doi.org/10.1016/j.jaccas.2020.05.095

[2] Yang, E., & Yang, S. (2020). Prior authorization: Overwhelming burden and critical need for reform. *JACC: Case Reports, 2*(10), 1466–1469. https://doi.org/10.1016/j.jaccas.2020.05.095

Through excessive utilization management strategies, health insurance companies are emphasizing that shareholders have priority over patients.

As Claudia's case demonstrates, corporations—healthcare insurers—are treating healthcare as a commodity, and that is a radical turnaround from the value of patient care my fellow doctors and I learned in medical school when we swore to uphold the Hippocratic Oath.

Should accessing the healthcare our insurance premiums pay for be so difficult or take so long? No.

CHAPTER 1

Anatomy of the Invisible Hand

The healthcare crisis in America is not a black problem or a white problem, a blue problem or a red problem. The healthcare crisis in America is a greed problem, a green problem. Unfortunately, this is not a 21st century problem, but a carryover from the last century.

Martin Luther King, Jr. made equity in healthcare a central pillar of his Poor People's Campaign because he believed that "of all forms of discrimination and inequality, injustice in health is the most shocking and inhuman."

As a result of the patient crises resulting from standard operating procedures of corporate healthcare insurers in the U.S., insurance companies have engendered deep resentment. The question plaguing both patients and physicians is, "How do I navigate this fractured system without losing my bank account and my mind?"

Luigi Mangione, the suspected perpetrator of the brutal December 4, 2024, murder of the UnitedHealthcare CEO, Brian Thompson, wrote on several occasions that "these parasites had it coming." He also wrote that corporate insurance was a "mafiosa [that] have gotten too powerful," and who "abuse the U.S. for immense profit."

Found at the scene of the fatal shooting of the Fortune 100 CEO were bullet casings inscribed with the words, "deny," "defend," and "depose." These tactics have been ascribed to insurance companies' avoidance of paying claims. Deny responsibility. Defend decisions. Depose claimants under oath. It was also no coincidence that at the time of his murder, the UnitedHealthcare CEO was entering a Manhattan hotel to host an important annual investors meeting. While the inscriptions on the bullet casings serve as a stark critique of industry accountability practices, it is important to acknowledge that resorting to murder and violence can never be justified as a means of expressing dissent or dissatisfaction. Calls for greater transparency and fairness should always be pursued through lawful, nonviolent avenues that respect the dignity and safety of every individual involved.

The power imbalance between large corporate institutions and patients who need healthcare has escalated due to the procedural nature of the tactics employed by these institutions to undermine patients' pursuit of payment for health insurance claims. When healthcare insurers refuse payment of claims, patients have two options: forego care or enter financial hardship. Additionally, the utilization management strategies employed by healthcare insurers are designed to result in the minimization of healthcare utilization. As a result, premiums are retained by companies, and investors' profit is maximized. By adjusting premiums upward and systematically paying out less, the industry has returned massive profits to shareholders, and companies like UnitedHealth Group have come to rank eighth (2024) on the Fortune Global 500.

Portraying commercial insurance companies as the antagonist risks oversimplifying a complex industry dynamic. After all, the patient-physician partnership requires the insurer to be not only a financing component, but also an independent observer holding physicians to account. This dual role ensures insurers act as both financial stewards and vigilant regulators, maintaining a balance that protects patients' interests while upholding clinical integrity and fostering accountability within the healthcare system. Right?

No, that is all wrong.

The power imbalance in healthcare presents a major obstacle that, for many patients, appears insurmountable. Instead of feeling covered and protected, patients feel like David standing before the giant, Goliath.

The invisible hand of healthcare's financiers, commercial insurers, is Goliath successfully halting patients' progress toward health, blocking patients from obtaining the healthcare they need, and physicians from properly practicing the profession for which they have trained for decades. Every day, individuals working for these corporations, many lacking medical qualifications, are manipulating healthcare behind the scenes with one objective: company profit.

The insights in these chapters reflect rigorous research and evidence-based perspectives on insurance, strengthening the argument I present. What follows is not mere opinion—it is the result of deliberate, comprehensive research into the complexities of insurance and its impact on healthcare. The perspectives presented here form a well-supported argument that challenges conventional thinking and invites you to consider the deeper truths behind the policies shaping patient care.

But before jumping in, let's first answer the question, "What is the invisible hand?" The "invisible hand" in healthcare is a play on Adam Smith's metaphor for the unseen forces that make a capitalist, or free market, for-profit healthcare system. The basic premise of the invisible hand metaphor is that the individual freedom to choose between for-profit healthcare offerings will result in the betterment of society. The term "invisible hand" first appeared in 1759 in the "Theory of Moral Sentiments," written by Scottish philosopher Adam Smith. It then reappeared in 1776 in "An Inquiry Into the Nature and Causes of the

Wealth of Nations," to describe how the markets motivate members of society to produce what is necessary, a system of mutual benefit.

However, on the cover of this book, we depict the current dystopian reality of the invisible hand in healthcare. A hand wielding the scalpel, cutting patients and providers with policies intended to bar the way to the advanced healthcare the United States of America has been known for since the early 1900s.

But the foundation for understanding the cause of the current state of America's healthcare and potential beneficial changes in the system rests on the question, "Why is America's healthcare in crisis?" The focus of this book is healthcare economics from the perspective of a private practice doctor.

And at the beginning of this chapter, I made a bold claim that what ails our nation's healthcare is not black or white, red or blue, but green, as in greed. And in 1966, Dr. Martin Luther King Jr. took the idea a step further to say, "injustice in health is ... inhuman."

For most people, the absence of health concerns is a form of liberation. Experiencing illness firsthand reveals a simple truth: health equals freedom. Illness strips away more than liberty—it erodes every part of our lives. If we're not healthy, we probably won't be happy. If America calls itself, "the land of the free," it must actively ensure that everyone enjoys the freedom that true health provides. Americans want to be healthy because we want to be happy: free to work, play with our children, travel, participate in sports, and simply live a pain-free life.

We want to be healthy because we want to leave a legacy for our children and their children. Poor health jeopardizes a person's ability to maintain steady employment. It can force individuals to take significant time off or settle for wages that barely cover basic living expenses, undermining financial stability and independence. If retirement savings are tied up in memory care or inpatient care because our insurance policy does not pay, we'll run through our nest egg faster than we can imagine. Then, instead of leaving a legacy, we'll leave a burden for the next generation.

We are familiar with all the "be healthy" slogans: "Prioritize your mental wellness." "Take charge in the fight against cancer." "Defy Alzheimer's with knowledge and action." "Own your health journey every day." "Healthy choices build a happier life." Certainly, the medical community wants to create the winning formula to shift individual healthcare thinking to prioritize preventive health, which includes diet, exercise, being nicotine-free, marijuana and THC-free, alcohol-minimum, and embracing a healthy lifestyle.

But what if you're obese and you just can't lose the weight? We have treated patients in our practice whose joint replacement surgeries were denied by insurance solely because of their obesity. In one case, instead of treating his arthritis, our patient was told by his insurance company to lose weight, even if it meant undergoing weight loss surgery.

When a thyroid disease patient contacted a Pittsburgh news station, I was asked to contribute commentary that reflects understanding and professional expertise. Her dilemma was that her insurance company refused to pay for the one medication that could treat her condition, prescribed by her endocrinologist, denying multiple appeals, leaving her with severe thyroid disease, untreated.

We physicians practice medicine by examining our patients and developing treatment plans based on our medical expertise, only to be told by an authorizing insurance company representative, "We are not going to pay." By reviewing publications, I gleaned an insider's analysis of how the invisible hand has operated on its unwilling victims, patients who pay premiums, like this thyroid disease patient.

In exploring the complex world of health insurance and American healthcare, I discovered on a range of compelling insider perspectives and authoritative analyses. Investigative journalism also sheds light on patients burdened by large medical bills while insurers profit. Together, these sources provide a critical foundation for understanding the forces shaping our healthcare landscape. To understand the crisis in our healthcare system, we must first listen to the voices insiders rarely share.

Many of the "insider perspectives" I reference come from the 2024 article in the *Intelligencer* entitled, *The Confessions of Health Insurance Executives*, written by Chris Stanton. I also cite a July 2021 article by Dr. Robert H. Shmerling in Harvard Medical School's *Harvard Health Publishing* entitled, *Is Our Health System Broken?* I was intrigued by the clear data presented in an investigative article published in the New York Times on April 7, 2024, written by Chris Hamby, *Patients Hit With Big Bills While Insurers Reap Fees*.

FDA commissioner, Dr. Marty Makary, in his book, *The Price We Pay: What Broke American Healthcare—and How to Fix It*, describes why healthcare has become a "bubble" and the elusive "money games" of the business of medicine. Lastly, I found great economic insights in *The Coming Healthcare Revolution: 10 Forces That Will Cure America's Health Crisis* by health executives David W. Johnson and Paul Kusserow, published in 2024.

Behind every policy and headline, unseen forces shape the future of American healthcare. What if the biggest secrets of the healthcare industry were staring us right in the face, hidden in plain sight? Each of these references sheds light on perspectives to which I would otherwise not have gained access. I am grateful to the authors and journalists who present the hidden economics of American healthcare.

The American Medical Association survey on prior authorization reported worsening patient outcomes due to exhaustive insurance company prior authorization requirements; 75% of patients abandoned their treatments because of obstacles associated with the prior authorization process.

Why would insurers implement stringent prior authorization policies that directly result in patient harm by causing patients to abandon their treatment plan?

Physicians are recommending reasonable healthcare treatments that can avert unnecessary complications and significantly improve the health of their patients while insurers are denying the care, creating poorer patient outcomes. In one case study, where patients observed were denied coverage for a cardiology medication, the patients who were denied coverage and discontinued treatment because of high copays had higher rates of acute coronary syndrome, coronary intervention, stroke, and cardiac arrest.

The use of prior authorizations to halt patient care has expanded so that surgeons who are performing emergent surgeries at trauma centers are being asked to obtain prior authorizations after the fact, or retroactively. Surgeons, like my partner Marc, performing emergent operations at trauma centers face the added administrative burden of securing prior authorizations retroactively, which complicates urgent care delivery and places undue strain on already critical, time-sensitive decision-making processes. "Healthcare is a weird thing where you don't want the customer to use your product," was how one exec put it.

It goes without saying that patients can be proactive and try to avoid denials by having a long-term perspective and not waiting for healthcare issues to arise. I absolutely recommend that we all engage in well-care, have regular screenings, and be fiscally conscientious about our healthcare.

Even still, we all must answer the question, "Is my insurance plan one that charges me an additional out-of-pocket cost associated with a colonoscopy, a mammogram, or a screening blood test?" Because insurers pass the cost of care along to the insured, the cost of regular checkups should be in our annual budget, as well as on our calendar.

In the *Intelligencer* article, each of the four insurance executives Stanton interviewed describes how the corporate insurers take medicine, the art and science of patient care, pull it away from providers, and use their financial leverage to cut the care our patients receive. And certainly, the research validates and supports everything I learned in our practice as survivors of the "Health Insurance Industrial Complex."

In *The Coming Healthcare Revolution*, Johnson and Kusserow describe the economics of the **financial incentive-patient need** imbalance. Corporations managing healthcare insurance are incentivized to reduce utilization of healthcare services while their subscribers, America's patients, need healthcare.

Americans are forecasted to spend over $5.6 trillion on healthcare in 2025 alone, reflecting a relentless surge that now accounts for nearly one-fifth of the nation's economy, a staggering increase that highlights the urgent need for reform. Annual premiums for family health rose from $13,871 in 2010 to an average of $24,000 in 2023, which constitutes a whopping 32% of median household income. Furthermore, out-of-pocket costs, separate from premium costs, are nearly $1,500 per person per year. And over 60% of Americans say they forego healthcare services because of cost.

While many Americans refused to get the care they needed because they could not pay, the former healthcare insurance executives who chose to speak out "all described stomach-churning encounters with greed that prompted them not only to leave the for-profit health-insurance industry but to question its premise." All four executives Stanton interviewed described how they manipulated the government. Does that mean the government is complicit?

The fact that all four executives Stanton interviewed admitted to manipulating the government does not conclusively prove government complicity, but it undeniably raises serious concerns about the effectiveness of regulatory oversight. It suggests a system vulnerable to influence and exploitation, where powerful industry players leverage lobbying, campaign contributions, and regulatory capture to shape policies in their favor. While the government may not actively condone such manipulation, these revelations highlight systemic weaknesses that allow corporate interests to circumvent rules meant to protect public welfare, calling for stronger transparency, accountability, and reforms to restore balance and trust.

Former Cigna executive Ron Howrigan's "come to Jesus" moment occurred shortly after his employer cut payment rates to obstetricians. Coincidentally, Howrigon's wife had a successful C-section. Before he left the operating room, his wife's obstetrician told him, "Next time you take money out of a doctor's pocket, remember today because I'm the one who was here."

Hamby, of The New York Times, says the collection formula for, "the insurance companies is simple: The smaller the [doctor] reimbursement, the larger their fee." He found that, "the largest insurer by revenue, UnitedHealthcare, has reaped an annual windfall of about $1 billion in fees from out-of-network savings programs...according to testimony by two of its executives." In 2023, a data analytics firm called Multiplan "told investors, it identified nearly $23 billion in bills from various insurers that it recommended not to be paid."

I was struck by the research, not because what I unearthed surprised me, but because my practice experience had also led me to this conclusion. How we discuss the financial issues strangling our healthcare system is not a discussion of why certain necessary medications are not covered by insurance, including $25,000 Hepatitis C medications, but a discussion of why it is so challenging to get prior authorization that 75% of patients abandon care.

Economists have devised a formula to measure the crisis at hand: the impact of the cost of healthcare. **The Healthcare Affordability Index** "reveals this obvious, but hidden truth: The very high cost of private health insurance contributes significantly to middle class stagnation." And even more glaringly, economists have also determined the obvious socioeconomic impact. Evidence shows that "the financial burden of paying for health insurance falls disproportionately on lower-income households whose stagnant wages have risen more slowly than their health insurance costs."[1]

An unnamed insurance company executive mentioned that insurance execs are largely insulated from their own policies. Stanton shares his reflections on an instance when an insurance colleague, "came to him when their spouse was diagnosed with cancer, 'petrified' that they wouldn't receive timely care through one of the insurer's own plans." These healthcare executives know they cannot save patients' lives, but through financial manipulation, they devise policies that may take a life or at least prevent one from getting the best care, and that happens over and over. "The financial incentive to deny care is at the core of the industry's rot, all four former executives argue."[2]

Chris Hamby, in the April 7, 2024, issue of The New York Times, describes the extent to which insurance companies like Aetna, Cigna, and UnitedHealthcare will go to use data analytics to decide how much providers will be paid, sometimes leaving insured patients with huge balances for emergency care. "But a New York Times investigation,

---

[1] Health Journalism. (2024, March). *Report shows rising insurance costs erode workers' earnings, increase disparities.* Association of Healthcare Journalists. Retrieved August 28, 2025, from https://healthjournalism.org/blog/2024/03/report-shows-rising-insurance-costs-erode-workers-earnings-increase-disparities/

[2] https://hc4us.org/the-health-care-executives-who-quit-over-greed-new-york-magazine/

based on interviews and confidential documents, shows that the insurance companies have a large and mostly hidden financial incentive to cut reimbursements as much as possible, even if it means saddling patients with large bills."

Admittedly, staying healthy can be a bigger challenge if we don't live in the right zip code. Social determinants of health are real. Several years ago, I participated in a state-wide leadership program. We examined many factors influencing our lives in the state of New Jersey, including education, climate change, and health. One month, we visited an underserved community in Newark, where we were given the weekly allowance families on public assistance have for a week's worth of groceries. I believe it was forty-five dollars.

We had to feed a family of four and shop only in stores within walking distance of our starting point. There were no supermarkets, only small local businesses, mom and pop shops, meaning prices were higher. It was challenging to plan meals with that amount of money while also making healthy choices. Were we going to buy rice or pasta? And what about vegetables? In the end, the only vegetables we could afford were canned selections. Cereal- what choice would the kids eat, and at the same time, could we eliminate choices with high sugar content?

We may read slogans like, "Live a healthy lifestyle." But if socioeconomic predeterminants make it almost impossible to do that, then what? Certainly, there should be no shaming of patients who come with what might appear to be a preventable illness. Perhaps they simply couldn't afford to drive to a supermarket to buy healthy but expensive fruits and vegetables.

But still, we must do something to address social determinants of health. History shows that change comes when people demand it. The system is changing, whether we want it to or not. It's up to us to ensure the change is to a model that works for patients, reducing the financial pressure associated with maintaining good health.

Is Our Healthcare System Broken? by Robert H. Shmerling, MD, assesses the financial burden of America's healthcare, saying that many people risk bankruptcy. "Healthcare prices vary widely, and it's nearly impossible to compare the quality or cost of your healthcare options—or even to know how big a bill to expect. And even when you ask lots of questions ahead of time and stick with recommended doctors in your health insurance network, you may still wind up getting a surprise bill. My neighbor did after knee surgery: even though the hospital and his surgeon were in his insurance network, the anesthesiologist was not." In his *Intelligencer* article, Stanton concludes that insurers' financial incentives are fundamentally at odds with patients' needs.

I took a closer look at whistleblower Wendell Potter's body of work and the advocacy he has led since leaving major healthcare insurance provider Cigna as Vice President for Corporate Communications. The landing page on his website says, "I'm Wendell Potter. I spent 20 years as a health insurance insider, running propaganda campaigns that benefited corporations. After seeing the corruption from the inside, I've dedicated my life to reforming the healthcare industry through education, advocacy, and speaking truth to power." Since the December 2024 killing of UnitedHealthcare CEO Brian Thompson, Potter has been "the go-to expert to help explain how insurance companies screw over patients."

In the aftermath of the attack on the nation's largest healthcare insurer's CEO, Brian Thompson, in broad daylight, Wendell Potter described the tactics the current executives would take with precision.

"No interviews with reporters except in the friendliest of circumstances. Write an op-ed for CEO Andrew Witty in the New York Times acknowledging that this is a difficult business but that the company will work to do right by Americans. Give lobbyists talking points to assuage Congress, and give account representatives separate talking points to placate employer customers who may be facing calls from their workers to switch providers. And of course, send out Witty to comfort anxious shareholders."[3]

Of course, UnitedHealthcare's corporate strategists followed Potter's playbook.

But Potter's additional comment to Stanton was chilling. "I'll assure you that the least important stakeholders are the people who are enrolled in their health plans. They're at the bottom of the pile."

With patients at the bottom of the pile, it becomes clear that the system's shortcomings not only marginalize the most vulnerable but also threaten the very integrity and sustainability of healthcare itself, demanding urgent and comprehensive reform.

This is the invisible hand with fingers entangled with managed government-backed health plans and insurance company investors, gripping the narrative. No one will escape the grip of our fractured healthcare system. In his book, Makary observed that, "behind the scenes, a gigantic industry emerged: buying, selling, and trading our medical services. Healthcare industry stakeholders are playing a game, marking up the price of medical care."

As a doctor, I surmised this was the case after 15 years of diligently caring for orthopedic patients from all walks of life. When I started my journey in medicine, I couldn't conceive that an industry sanctioned by state and national government to act as the financial instrument for the standard of American healthcare would prioritize share price and profit

---

[3] Witty, A. (2024, December 13). The healthcare system is flawed. Let's fix it. The New York Times. Wile, R. (2025, January 16). *UnitedHealth CEO says U.S. health system 'needs to function better'*. NBC News. Retrieved from https://www.nbcnews.com/business/business-news/unitedhealth-ceo-says-us-health-system-needs-function-better-rcna187980

margins over cancer care, emergent C-sections, and urgent ankle fracture treatment. Only when it was personal, when a family member or a child was affected, did these executives demonstrate remorse for their reprehensible approach to utilization management and sketchy reimbursement practices. Through interviews and publications, these executives provided valuable insight into an invisible hand without a true moral compass.

When I received my MBA from Oxford University, I was the only medical doctor in my cohort. After I was selected to give a commencement speech, I asked the student representatives, "What kind of speech do you want this to be? Do you want a gratitude or thank-you speech, or do you want it to be a go forth speech?"

They said, "We'll handle the gratitude. You do the go forth speech."

Having just lived through the COVID-19 pandemic and simultaneously completing this potentially life-changing business course, as well as doing it at Oxford University, founded in 1096 and one of the oldest educational institutions in the world, I was inspired to take a historical perspective.

I looked at the resources and various perspectives of historical figures. We called COVID-19 a pandemic, but it wasn't the first global illness the world had endured. Back in 1096, they called them plagues.

I said, "This is how we fit in the history of this institution. Business touches every sector of our society, so we have an obligation to contribute to the world."

Given where we studied and stood, at the 900-year-old Oxford University, it's no surprise that, on that day, I drew upon the poetic wisdom of Shakespeare, specifically referencing the play, *Julius Caesar*.

"In William Shakespeare's Julius Caesar, Brutus describes to Cassius the value of recognizing and seizing opportunity, even in unsettled times. He says,

'There is a tide in the affairs of men,
Which, taken at the flood, leads on to fortune.
Omitted, all the voyage of their life
Is bound in shallows and miseries.
On such a full sea are we now afloat.
And we must take the current when it serves or lose our ventures.'

I went on to say, "During the last eighteen months, we buried friends, colleagues, relatives, jobs, and our old way of life. Sometimes when you're in a dark place, you, too, can think you've been buried, but you realize you've been planted."

What I said then is even more significant now. After the horrors of 2020, I wanted my fellow graduates to go forth. I wanted all of us to go out into the world and make a difference: to change the world for the better.

That is also what I want us to do now.

This invisible hand has nearly doubled insurance premiums and out-of-pocket costs for patients. Corporate insurers are taking one-third of Americans' annual income for care that they don't want patients, as customers, to use.

This was not the world I signed up for when I chose my career in medicine.

CHAPTER 2

From Harvard to Hopkins to Healthcare

Before I started this journey, I had no concept of the medical landscape or the invisible hand that would take my dream hostage. Now I understand the power imbalance in healthcare presents an obstacle that appears insurmountable.

My medical journey began early one spring morning as I walked over the uneven 17th century cobblestones from my dorm, in the Old Radcliffe Quad, to Harvard Square and the taxicab stand, my suitcase bumping along behind me.

Harvard had been home for four years, and that morning it was time for me to leave Cambridge and realize my dream of becoming a physician, of making a difference in people's lives. I felt certain of my future career path, but avenues have a way of taking unexpected dips and curves when you think they should run in a straight line.

I had prepared my whole life for this path, constantly improving myself, achieving better grades. I took the MCAT more than once, striving to be an applicant good enough to get into medical school. I studied for my undergraduate courses with knife-edge precision. My maroon Day-Timer held a 'round-the-clock schedule accurate to the minute, as I was determined to become a better time manager. I also aspired to be a well-liked team member who brought value to group projects in my engineering major. I became a top performer with equally high expectations. I volunteered clinically, taking the bus to Boston City Hospital. It was the height of the AIDS epidemic, and the nurses on the pediatric floor made sure I was covered from head to toe before I assumed my post in a rocking chair where I would hold tiny babies who missed their mothers. Their weak cries and abnormal convulsions belied an addiction to the drugs their mothers had ingested while pregnant.

That morning, I wheeled my suitcase down Garden Street in Cambridge to the taxicab stand. I was on my way to Logan Airport to catch a flight to Baltimore for my interview at The Johns Hopkins University School of Medicine. Entering the historical Marburg Pavilion the following morning from the immaculately landscaped courtyard, the historical main entry to *The* Johns Hopkins Hospital, I passed underneath the outstretched arms of Christus Consolator, the 10.5-foot statue of Jesus Christ. The myriad small, folded pieces of paper and flowers strewn at its feet were evidence that each day, countless prayers, blessings, and thanksgivings are made at the feet of the inspiring marble sculpture.

Then, I noticed the words inscribed at the statue's base, the quote from Matthew 11:28, "Come unto me, and I will give you rest."

So here I was staring at Jesus towering over me with outstretched arms on my way to the interview at *The* Johns Hopkins. I'd dreamed about my future career since I was five and my mother told me I was going to be a doctor. I never doubted it. I had a natural aptitude for math and science, and, as a "gifted and talented" student, attended a math, science, and computer magnet school.

Medicine seemed the right choice because I would be able to work in the sciences while also getting to know people and improving the lives of patients. As a doctor, I knew I was going to contribute to society. I did not want to deal with the common dilemma of "doing the right thing" versus doing my job. I wouldn't have to make the sort of compromises I might be forced into if I chose a career in another field, like law or public service.

Johns Hopkins School of Medicine turned out to be a wonderful choice. I didn't realize until I was in my surgical residency at another institution, the tremendous respect Johns Hopkins afforded its students. The motto of Hopkins Medical School is "See one. Do one. Teach one," a methodology of teaching, learning skills, and best practices through direct observation of a task. It also emphasizes caring for the patient and not standing idly by. The motto resonated with me profoundly.

Even as a medical student, I was diagnosing patients with serious conditions. I had the opportunity to write my own note in the chart and sign it with my name, followed by the letters MS (medical student) and a Roman numeral representing my medical school year. If any other medical team wanted more information, they came directly to me. Johns Hopkins Medicine fostered a culture of excellence. Everyone worked long hours, but we gave each patient our best.

The emergency room was my third clinical rotation. The AIDS and opioid crises were simultaneously in full swing in Baltimore. Intravenous drug users who resorted to subcutaneous injection of drugs because their veins were no longer accessible frequently arrived at the emergency department with skin infections that needed debridement. One ER shift, I was fully gowned with my face shield in place, irrigating an abscess for one such patient. Behind me, I could hear a resident from another service complain, "Why are my tax dollars being spent treating patients like this? We shouldn't have to do this work, let alone bear the cost!"

I don't agree, but I understand the question. I also appreciate that behind the question lies a disconnect between the physician and patient. The disconnect is compensation.

I hate to use the cliche, but saying the "system" is the problem is the only way of summarizing our circumstances accurately. Those insurance companies that provide compensation want us, patient and doctor, to turn against one another.

Where Marc and I practice, in Bayonne, New Jersey, our patients are predominantly working class, and insurance is essential to cover the cost of care. In contrast, when I was training for orthopedic surgery in Manhattan, patients often dealt with their insurance privately, and institutions, like hospitals, didn't have to handle the administrative nightmares associated with waiting for insurance reimbursement. On the other hand, our Bayonne population comprises a mix of insurance, called a payor mix,[1] where many of our patients depend on their insurance to afford their healthcare.

We need the capacity to accept and deal with insurance companies. And that's where the challenges to our practice's bottom line lie. That's where my idealistic vision of patient care hit the wall of reality. Certainly, we were benefiting from the community economically, but we also wanted to be beneficiaries *to* the community. But the fact is, the healthcare insurance system is the antagonist and makes the practice of healthcare challenging.

The insurance claims process today is all about obfuscation. When I went to medical school, I thought I was going to be free to care for my patients. I wasn't going to have to deal with the moral dilemmas that so many other professions must face. But then, I naively entered this system rife with those very moral dilemmas I thought I would never experience.

---

[1] Allen, J. (2024, June 10). *Understanding payer mix. What I've Learned As A Hospital Medical Director*. Retrieved August 29, 2025, from https://hospitalmedicaldirector.com/understanding-payer-mix/

The health insurance benefits provided to workers were supposed to improve the quality of life, but look at the overburdened providers; their quality of life is not improving. We're told we should just be seeing more patients, one every 10 to 15 minutes. We are expected to complete more charts. And doctors employed by hospitals are pressured by the threat that their privileges will be suspended because charts are incomplete. This is why many MDs routinely pay more attention to the electronic medical record than to the patient. How does that improve the quality of patient care?

Choosing a career in medicine is a sacrifice. Freedom? The insurance companies are at the point of believing they own the doctors caring for their customers, and they're not wrong. We, doctors, should be able to care for our patients without reservation, but in reality, that doesn't happen. The system today seems to operate for the sake of making insurance shareholders wealthy. Five major healthcare insurance companies operate in the United States. Since 1980, their share price has skyrocketed.[2] Brian Thompson, who was killed in midtown Manhattan in December 2024, was the CEO of UnitedHealthcare, a $580 billion company. Should any healthcare company be that rich? What strategies did they employ to arrive at that valuation?

The March 2025 *Intelligencer* article I referenced earlier cites former Cigna executive Ron Howrigon, who recalled debating cost-cutting measures with his colleagues. When he joked that they could cut costs by releasing in-network specialists, the CEO, Mark Bertolini, said they needed to "execute a few hostages." In other words, target expensive specialists and solo practices, perhaps practices like ours.

---

[2] Hamby, C. (2024, April 7). *Patients hit with big bills while insurers reap fees.* *The New York Times.*https://www.nytimes.com/2024/04/07/us/health-insurance-medical-bills.html

In the early days, I had to learn to build a successful private practice, including a whole new vocabulary invented by insurance companies. Very little of what I learned related to the practice of medicine, but instead, I mastered interactions with insurance companies and the finance of medicine.

As I wrote this manuscript, I found that many authors understood the complexities of healthcare finance. However, I found few who could empathize with the injustice and inequality that resulted from this healthcare system.

This situation must change.

CHAPTER 3

The Fallacies

In conversations with other healthcare providers, it has become clear to me that a large contributor to the persistence of our ongoing issues with the U.S. health system is the American public's lack of information. Through no fault of their own, many have ascribed to common misconceptions about healthcare and believe in fallacies that must be examined and disproved. These fallacies are perpetuated, in part, by the media campaigns described by Wendell Potter's book, *Deadly Spin*.

Fallacy number one: Doctors are rich, so why should we care?

Fallacy number two: Hospitals are rich, so why should we care?

In other words, the price of healthcare is ultrahigh, bankrupting the common people, because doctors and hospitals are making huge profits.

This is far from the truth.

Everything we do in medicine is billed with a Current Procedural Terminology (CPT) code, and the reimbursements for care associated with CPT codes change based on zip code or payor. If a healthcare institution is providing care for a significant number of self-pay, no-pay, or government-backed insurance patients, that institution may need to balance its books, resulting in a higher price tag for the CPT codes. These under-resourced facilities are banking on being fully reimbursed for the patients who have good insurance to cover the patients that don't have insurance or have insurance that typically underpays.

We all understand the inhumanity of healthcare injustice that Dr. King was trying to communicate during his Poor People's campaign. Unjust socioeconomic disparities are pervasive. In America, the quality of every aspect of life is based on our location, our zip code: education, tax rates, and certainly, healthcare. If I perform a procedure in one county that has wealthy patients with a high median income, I will likely get reimbursed more than if I do the same surgery 10 miles away in a zip code where the median income is lower, with a more economically diverse patient population. The balance of payments should be the opposite, because taking care of patients who can't afford to see their doctor often, and who may have serious health problems and more complicated concerns, will likely entail more work for me. But, instead of being paid for the complexity, physicians and facilities get paid less because of the zip code where care is provided.

This is an issue across healthcare systems. Medicare and Medicaid, specifically the latter, pay a fraction of the cost of the medical care patients receive. The CEO of Scripps Healthcare describes the context for supporting safety-net facilities.[1] For example, if a pediatric patient comes in with an ankle fracture and she is covered by insurance that underpays, and we fix the fracture with open reduction internal fixation,[2] Medicaid may not cover the full cost of the plate and screws, let alone the operating room costs, or the pre- and post-operative care.

---

[1] The US hospital system is approaching a financial breaking point - Becker's Hospital Review | Healthcare News & Analysis. (n.d.). https://www.beckershospitalreview.com/finance/the-u-s-hospital-system-is-approaching-a-financial-breaking-point/

[2] A procedure where the bone is surgically exposed, realigned, and held in place with internal hardware like plates, screws, or rods to ensure proper healing.

Most likely, the medical institution will operate in a deficit, not fully recovering its costs because it will be underpaid by Medicaid.

If we have an emergency room patient with Medicare health insurance, presenting with a hip fracture, the medical institution or hospital may break even if the operation goes well, but if there is a complication, which occurs not infrequently with elderly patients, then Medicare reimbursements will not fully cover the cost of care, including the surgeon's time, the implants, hip screws, or prosthesis, and any prescription medication the patient may need for the injury or another pre-existing, unrelated condition.

Contrary to the false public perception, hospitals are not rich. To continue viability for the patients they serve, hospitals are trying to balance their books.

In our practice, Marc and I are not solely trying to balance our books; we are focused on consistently getting our accounts receivable paid accurately, at fair health rates, and in a timely manner. We are forever dependent on the private insurers to pay what we charge, and unfortunately, we are increasingly finding that insurers may not pay what it costs us to see our patients. Our practice is being reimbursed less and less for our services, in-office X-rays, and elective surgeries, as well as for office hours.

When Marc started his practice, before I joined him, he said, "Seeing patients during office hours is the bread and butter of the practice; that's our operating revenue. The surgeries are just icing on the cake."

By the time I joined, that circumstance was on a reverse trajectory. Today, for our private practice, the reimbursement schedule is the exact opposite. If we didn't do surgeries at all, we would not be able to continue operations. The amount insurance companies pay for office visits does not cover the total cost of patient care.

So, no, doctors and hospitals are not rich.

And again, let me ask the question: why is it that when patients present to an institution, the cost for a particular service varies depending on which facility a patient visits?

Fallacy number three: Insurers are trustworthy.

I've covered this, but it bears repeating. People tend to trust insurers because doctors and hospitals are forced to ask for reimbursement in the form of deductibles and copays at the time of service. Doctors and hospitals are the face the patient sees when making out-of-pocket payments mandated by their insurance; therefore, doctors are the "bad guys" asking for patients' money.

The fact is that the bad guy is the insurance company demanding the patient pay pocket money beyond the insurance premium. However, to get paid for health services rendered, the provider must be the one to collect the copay and deductible. Logically, the patient thinks, "I have to pay more because the doctor or hospital is charging too much." That line of thinking leads right into fallacy number one, fallacy number two, as well as fallacy number three.

As I wrote earlier, gatekeepers rationing care and making utilization management decisions through insurance companies are not bound to patients by the Hippocratic Oath. Insurers comprise a practical financial instrument used to pay for healthcare. But more and more, insurers are encroaching on the decision-making abilities of the Hippocratic oath-bound health care providers, specifically through utilization management.

Additionally, the physicians who are bound by the Hippocratic Oath are tied up or restricted by the prior authorization practices employed by insurance companies not bound by that oath. When I obtain a prior authorization for an MRI or for surgery, I may be asked to have a dialogue with someone who has a medical degree or even someone who has completed an orthopedic surgery residency. However, I am mindful that the medical doctor I'm speaking with is not bound to my patient by the Hippocratic Oath. The insurance company's doctors' decisions are dictated by the corporate regulations, protocols, and procedures of the insurance company that pays his or her salary.

If my patient is diagnosed with cancer, the insurance company that provides my patient's healthcare coverage, and the individual who will grant or deny the prior authorization for the patient's course of treatment, have no ultimate responsibility for saving my patient's life.

When we bring a patient into our practice, they become part of our extended family. Marc and I feel an obligation to the patient. We insist that the care we provide is of the same quality we would give to a member of our immediate family. We go to bat for our patients. We get on the telephone with the gatekeepers at the insurance companies, and we have conversations with individuals who couldn't care less. We plead, we call again, and we try again, until every avenue is exhausted.

Every person in our practice is invested. We feel we must get on the telephone again and then again, and it can be demeaning. (Why we must make our appeals by telephone is another question altogether.) Our motivation to persist is the possibility of improving or saving our patients' lives. That is not the gatekeeper at the insurer's motivation.

Where utilization management strategies and prior authorization requirements are concerned, insurers are not always trustworthy.

To begin to solve the myriad issues I've presented, I suggest that we need to rethink the entire zip code dilemma. This is a very concrete change we can make to the system. Similarly, we need to look at the CPT codes and the reimbursement per CPT code. Instead of choosing an arbitrary reimbursement, government-backed insurances should look at what's happening in the market: costs of staff, supplies, instruments, and instrumentation. This data determines the actual cost of care. What exactly does a hip replacement prosthesis and the patient's associated pre- and post-operative care cost? That should be calculated more precisely to reflect fair reimbursement, and it's not. Cost of care must be part of the calculation.

In 2023, 17.6% of the U.S. Gross Domestic Product (GDP) was spent on healthcare, with Medicare and Medicaid accounting for 21% and 18% of total health spending, respectively.[3] Commercial priorities like pharmaceuticals and premiums are escalating spending, while those providing care are operating with minimal margin. The government knows it's underpaying providers, but has chosen to let the medical facilities pick up the slack. As I said in an earlier chapter, the government is complicit with insurance companies.

If the government knows it's underpaying, how can it expect the nation's healthcare facilities to remain solvent? The government is relying on private insurers to overpay to cover the facility's losses due to underpayment on the government side. However, the reality is that the private insurers are no longer overpaying, and that spells trouble for the hospitals.

Now, add another layer of managed Medicaid and managed Medicare: government insurance administered through private insurers. They, too, underpay based on Medicaid and Medicare rates. On top of that, managed Medicare and Medicaid programs practice utilization management to collect more money from the federal government, pocketing a chunk of it, and limiting the services they allow healthcare providers to perform and patients to receive. And again, the result is the same: patients who have commercial insurance are being charged more by institutions to make up for the deficit.

Opening up this system for close inspection is like going into an abdominal surgery, thinking the colon cancer you're operating on is limited to a specific location in the bowel, but, during the operation, it

---

[3] Centers for Medicare & Medicaid Services. (2024). *2023 National health expenditure fact sheet* [Data set]. CMS. Retrieved August 29, 2025, from https://www.cms.gov/data-research/statistics-trends-and-reports/national-health-expenditure-data/nhe-fact-sheet

becomes clear that the cancer is more invasive than the preoperative imaging indicated. And you realize, "Oh, this case is much more involved than I thought." We call it a "peek and shriek." You look at the damage and the tumor and think, "I'm not ready for this. Let's sew the patient up, make a better operative plan, and come back another day."

Unfortunately, we don't have a peek and shriek option with our healthcare system. We must operate on it now.

I've learned that the keys to navigating America's health system are written on Luigi Mangione's shell casings. Deny. Defend. Depose.

Deny. Avoid denials. Partner with your physician. "They" want us to turn against one another. Don't vent your frustrations from interacting with your insurance carrier on your doctor. Defend. Attack the defense of the patients' "last" decisions by being vocal and using patient relations channels to express your concerns. As a last resort, consider changing insurance. Depose. Self-advocate even if it means going to court. Don't wait until it's life or death, until it's too late.

This system has survived a long time, but it's proving to be economically unfeasible. The healthcare insurers have arrived at a place where their benchmark is the level of underpayment offered by the government, through Medicare and Medicaid. Aligning private insurance reimbursements with those programs leaves many healthcare facilities with a deficit, especially when a covered patient needs more costly, hi-tech care. But then, through the mechanisms of utilization management, more and more patients are being denied the care they need. If patients do get access to care through prior authorization, the insurer can say, "But prior authorization wasn't a guarantee of payment."

The solution? With the help of AI, the government could begin to institute real-time surveys in healthcare systems across the country to quantify the real cost of implants, surgical procedures, and patient care and determine a more accurate reimbursement schedule.

Unfortunately, rather than raising the reimbursements for healthcare encounters, the state and federal governments are doing the exact opposite. If they cut even more, we will find ourselves in uncharted territory. The desperation of healthcare institutions brings the COVID days to mind when we just didn't know what we didn't know. We knew something bad was happening, and a catastrophe was escalating, but we were all still open for business.

Is the situation hopeless?

At the time, I certainly felt that way. I didn't have an answer then, only exhaustion and uncertainty.

CHAPTER 4

The Learning Curve

Life has a way of shifting.

Six weeks after my son's birth, after taking time to heal and to bond with him, I went straight back into my chief year of residency, and then into practice with my husband. While I entered the practice as an attending doctor and surgeon, I also wanted to understand how our practice remained viable. How did we generate our income? How did we interact with the payors, whether they were Workers' Compensation, private commercial insurers, or patients who simply paid cash?

I needed to know the business side because I have a strong inclination to understand the constituent parts of a project or a business endeavor. I need to be able to transparently visualize how all the parts work together.

I wanted to grasp the full picture before delegating responsibilities, right down to the day-to-day details. I approached Betty, the office manager, with my request. "Over the next several weeks, let's have a few breakfasts together, and you can explain things to me. Give me a sense of the history of the practice. Tell me your understanding of how things work, and take me around to meet some of the referring doctors. I would also like to meet some of the physical and occupational therapists to whom we refer our patients."

In other words, I was one of "those people." A pain in the butt? Maybe, but I was excited and all in. "Just show me what you know and who you know," I told Betty. "Show me what this practice environment in Hudson County is like."

I looked to her to clearly inform me of the dynamics of the practice, and she was terrific. In her little red Volkswagen Jetta, she drove me to the offices of various doctors and therapists. We talked in the car, with me asking a lot of questions, which she tried her best to answer. She explained as much as she could about the politics between different doctors' groups, and our practice's history with the doctors from whom we were renting our main office space.

When doctors Donna and Jonathan left the orthopedic group, Marc received more than a practice. He also inherited a leasing relationship with the two older doctors who owned the building in Springfield and another in Bayonne, where Marc was doing most of his work, and where I joined him. Betty explained those details and gave me a great picture of the general landscape as well as the "people" side of the business.

Unfortunately, I soon discovered that her grasp of the financial and economic side of the practice was not as strong as her analysis of the practice politics. Another problem was this feeling that we were beholden to the doctors we rented from. They weren't running our practice, but we also weren't just paying them rent. They provided our X-ray technicians and exerted a significant amount of control, not by directing our day-to-day operations, but by influencing our practice's standard operating procedures. If there was a conflict between our staff and theirs, theirs took priority. If issues arose between our utilization of space and theirs, they made the final decisions. The partners we rented from also rented space to another doctor in their building. So essentially, four separate doctors' offices operated in one large space. Four, because the owner/partners each had their own practice. Their influence was both tangible and intangible.

Even years later, when we decided to purchase office space in Bayonne, informing them of our move almost felt like we were asking for permission. I'm sure there was no ill will on their part, and maybe some of the influence was simply the dynamic of a relationship between older, paternalistic doctors and younger, less experienced doctors. To some extent, that could have been the psychology at play.

I also suspect I felt the paternalism of the relationship dynamic more than Marc did. Because I was a woman? Perhaps. It was a factor that couldn't be ruled out.

The relationships with the two partners who owned our office space were an important part of my understanding of how our practice worked. Knowing our staff and everyone's role was also key. And that is how, when I tried to decipher the cause and effect of our processes and systems, Betty presented me with a Venn diagram instead of a straight, clear line from A to B. I simply wanted to understand what happened after a patient walked into our office. Where did patients have touch points with each member of the staff? With whom? What was the role of the business staff versus that of the medical assistants conducting office hours? What were the office staff members' levels of expertise? What were each individual's strengths and weaknesses? Was their level of compensation based on their experience, contribution, and the number of hours they worked?

Basically, I was studying for a mini, on-the-job MBA, including running the HR side of the business. But try as I might, I could not seem to get Betty to produce a schematic of a linear process. Instead, I had a pile of circles that occasionally overlapped. It took a while for me to even begin to fully grasp the deficit in understanding. The question I asked earlier began plaguing me, "How do I navigate this fractured system without losing my bank account and my mind?"

A small practice operates very differently from a large healthcare organization. As a resident, I was part of the busiest orthopedic hospital in the world, providing patient care in every sub-specialty in the field of orthopedic surgery. Many patients paid cash, so the attending surgeons rarely had to deal with the nuances of commercial insurance.

I had no formal, academic preparation for the administrative side of medicine, and maybe that was to my benefit. If I'd known what I was about to tackle, it may have seemed too daunting to even try. My level of ignorance probably placed me in good stead, and kept me diving deeper and deeper, blissfully unaware of what I would unearth next.

While I was on this steep learning curve, I was also seeing patients three days a week and doing surgery the other two days. I had a full schedule of patients that I operated on while also assisting Marc with some of his surgeries as we handled elective and emergent cases at four separate hospital facilities.

At this point, handling orthopedic cases was something I could manage with some ease. The major challenge remained unearthing the inner workings of the private practice. Betty's view of our practice's operations and her take on the financial side of things was incomplete. She also tended to be responsive to our income and bank balance, instead of staying one step ahead.

My business philosophy was quite different from Betty's. I believe that if the process is correct, the outcome will be consistent, predictable, and right. As I examined how we functioned in our office, I wanted to understand our processes and how we could be more consistent. I thought that once we overcame this hurdle and became more efficient, our revenue stream would also be more consistent. I thought we could overcome the challenges of inconsistent revenue by working smarter.

To reach my goal, we hired Michael Sanders, a consultant, who effectively filled the role of efficiency expert. Not surprisingly, we got significant pushback from the staff. They were a collegial group, but they also weren't overly concerned with being more "efficient."

Our consultant wanted to know how much time the intake staff spent on patient telephone calls and precisely how we were taking clinical messages. He looked at the number of staff we had, their roles and responsibilities, and how they spent their time. We had five people in the back office just answering phones, making appointments, and only one sorting billing and collections. We had three medical assistants helping us with office hours and communicating with patients. In addition, we had a physician assistant and an office manager.

Betty and several other staff members asked, "Why are we doing this? Why do we have to answer Michael's questions? Why do we have to log our telephone calls? What is the purpose of this analysis? We don't understand how this is going to help run the practice."

But I needed to know. I couldn't get the answers directly from the staff, and I had to have someone get that information for me. How else was I going to get a thorough understanding of the business operations?

I was approaching this from an efficiency perspective, not from a people's. If I had approached it from a people's perspective right from the beginning, I would have realized quickly that what I really needed was several new staff members who were amenable to doing things more efficiently. I would have asked each member of our organization directly if they were willing to streamline their roles and responsibilities so that the organizational chart made sense, instead of presenting a Venn diagram consisting of overlapping circles.

Not surprisingly, some of our staff ultimately chose to leave because I wasn't about to go away, and we had committed to streamlining the way we operated the practice. The office staff would need clearly delineated roles and responsibilities. Based on our efficiency expert's recommendations, we would have to be more aware of how we communicated with patients on the telephone and how we managed our telephone etiquette and interactions, even with the insurance companies. Most importantly, we would answer the telephone. Putting phone lines on service was not going to be part of our practice culture.

Michael's consultant's report was part of our justification for letting people go, particularly in the back office. Betty was the first to go, but her departure was by her own choosing.

She was a good person who created a pleasant working environment and was very helpful to me, but she was also the kind of person who had difficulty with the details. For example, she would order office supplies we really didn't need. It took us years just to go through her supply of message pads. She ensured that bills got paid and pursued reimbursement payments when we needed the revenue, but not consistently. I wanted to know the monthly and weekly totals of our accounts receivable and payable. I aspired to operate in a predictable, fiscally responsible way.

To this day, people want to know why our medical practice does not operate on credit. Why should we? Why is that even normal for a small organization such as ours?

Marc and I had a vision. We wanted to create an orthopedic practice where anyone would feel comfortable the minute they stepped into the waiting room. I thought of us as a "sleeper" practice, meaning you might not see us on flashy billboards around town, but you would definitely hear about us through word of mouth and community referrals. Then, when you found us, you'd be so glad you did.

We wanted to wow our patients with our care, but not in a showy way. We intended to gain their trust. We even focused on our physical space, wanting it to reflect our vision. We painted it in calming blues and kept everything spotlessly clean, neat, and uncluttered. We made sure our patients knew that wherever we took them for surgery, they would receive cutting-edge care.

It was also important to us to be open with our patients and communicate with them clearly and effectively. Educating patients was and continues to be important to us. We tell them, "This is what you have," and we show them their films, which at first were on X-ray boxes in every room, and today, are presented digitally on a laptop where they can also view their MRIs. We don't do MRIs in our offices, but we do X-rays and always show them both.

We believe that if we inform and educate our patients, they will make the best decisions for themselves. Orthopedic conditions tend not to be life-threatening, so we really want patients to know all their options and make their own decisions. We believe we are partners with our patients. We can give them our best recommendations, but ultimately, the decision about how to proceed with their care is always theirs.

We won't push our patients to have surgery. Obviously, if we're looking at revenue generation, the more surgeries we perform, the more money we will make. But making money is not our primary goal. Nor should it be the goal of any doctor or surgeon.

Our primary aim is to partner with our patients, be a positive influence in their lives, and allow them to make educated decisions about their healthcare.

Some of those decisions are difficult. We had one patient who had developmental dysplasia of the hip[1] (DDH) as well as mild cerebral palsy.[2] However, she was highly functional, a single mother doing her best for herself and her son. I can only describe her personality as jubilant. But

---

[1] A condition where the hip socket is too shallow, failing to fully cover the ball-shaped head of the thigh bone.

[2] A permanent group of movement disorders caused by abnormal development or damage to a developing brain, affecting muscle tone, movement, and coordination.

the DDH was causing her great distress. Her hip socket was malformed and shallower than it should have been, and so, with time, she experienced wearing down of the cartilage, causing arthritis and severe pain.

We performed hip replacement surgery, and things went well. Then she developed an infection, and even through staged revision of her total hip replacement and treatment of her infection with intravenous antibiotics, she was always happy, greeting me every six weeks or so when she came into the office with a big smile and, "How are you doing, Dr. U?"

She brightened our entire office with her smile and positive attitude, even when she was in pain. She did well after the infection cleared up, but then it came back again, and then again. We never gave up. Together we fought against her disease even as the complications continued. But she never stopped trusting us, and she never lost her smile. She understood that challenges occur, even with the best that orthopedic medicine has to offer.

She was wonderful to work with, but it was also hard for all of us. When you have a beautiful patient, you want things to go perfectly for them, and, in her case, it didn't. But because of the way we operate our practice and how we built a rapport with her, she trusted us.

That is our practice philosophy. We work hard to create that trust through being honest and doing our best. Always.

CHAPTER 5

Sweat, Sacrifice, and Hard Work

In February 2006, I became pregnant with our second child. It was only my second year in the practice, and I couldn't have been busier. Marc was the acting chief of orthopedic surgery at Mt. Vernon Medical Center, so we were zigzagging back and forth between Newark, Springfield, Jersey City, Bayonne, and Secaucus; five different locations almost every day.

Marc and I faced challenges on multiple fronts during this time. As the acting chief of orthopedic surgery at Mt. Vernon Medical, he wasn't fully running his own department. Orthopedics was considered a division of general surgery, and the chief of general surgery had the ultimate decision-making power regarding orthopedic care, although he had a more administrative role, splitting his time between those duties and looking after patients. He also had access to billing records and understood the contributions orthopedic surgery made to his department. He managed the call schedule, the orthopedic surgeons, and issues that might come up with them.

His main challenges at Mt. Vernon were organizational.

At other facilities, orthopedic attendings were provided 24-hour coverage by physician assistants (PAs) who were available to help with surgeries and manage inpatients. But at Mt. Vernon, the PAs only worked weekdays, during an 8-4 or 9-5 shift. Where other departments, including general surgery, had residents, orthopedics did not. If an emergency or even a routine question presented regarding post-surgical inpatients after hours, the attending orthopedic surgeon was the go-to. Each time a surgical patient had to stay overnight, Marc or I would receive multiple calls from the nursing staff.

For Marc, taking an orthopedic trauma call at Mt. Vernon was both intense and demanding. Demanding because he might receive a call every couple of hours during the night, often about issues he shouldn't have had to deal with, and intense because he often found himself repeating tasks. For example, an order for the patient to receive Tylenol might be on their chart, but he'd get a call asking if the patient should receive medication. More than once, Marc said, "I feel like I'm in residency again."

Today, there are hospitalists and physician assistants who are available to handle those issues, but at the time, the potential for burnout was high, especially if the patient had serious or complicated health problems in addition to orthopedic issues.

Mt. Vernon had additional challenges that some other hospitals in the area didn't experience, at least not to the same extent. Marc and I might want to perform three total joint replacements in one day on three different patients. Even with two surgeons, we found it virtually impossible to start at 7:30 a.m. and finish before 8 p.m. With reasonably experienced staff, our actual time in the operating room would be about an hour or perhaps 15 minutes more per case. Theoretically, if we were working efficiently, we should have completed all three cases by 3 p.m., and that's a generous estimate. But we rarely finished before 8 p.m., five hours later than efficiency would dictate.

Why?

Part of the reason was how the operating rooms were managed in terms of turnover time. A case booked for 7:30 a.m. probably would not get into the operating room until 8:15 a.m. And then we'd wait for the patient to receive anesthesia, and that could be an issue. We preferred our arthroplasty[1] patients to receive a combination of general and regional anesthesia, so that when they woke up from the general anesthesia, they weren't immediately in severe pain. The regional anesthesia to the operative extremity would wear off gradually, with breakthrough pain handled by narcotic medications. So, we preferred to work with an anesthesiologist who was comfortable administering regional anesthesia in combination with a lighter version of general anesthesia, giving the patient a smoother, less painful recovery. That conversation, and the preparation of the patient, inevitably took up precious time, and it could well be 9 a.m. before our surgery actually got started.

Once the surgery was done, we'd roll the patient to the recovery room, write our orders, and head back to the operating room to prepare the next case. In many medical facilities, they would have already been pretty far along with turning over the room, cleaning, and preparing the trays for the next case. At Mt. Vernon, we often found ourselves waiting, sometimes as long as an hour or an hour-and-a-half, for this process to be completed.

And that's how three surgeries stretched to 12 hours.

At that time, in 2005–2006, it was frustrating. Now, these types of delays have become normal in many hospitals. Many facilities have staffing shortages, and because of that, many are using "travelers." A traveler is not a full-time hospital employee. They go from hospital to hospital, from operating facility to operating facility, some traveling across the country with serial engagements from 3–6 months.

---

[1] An orthopedic surgical procedure where damaged or diseased joint surfaces are replaced with an artificial component (prosthesis) to relieve pain and restore function.

A traveler new to a facility doesn't know where anything is or how the system works in each new hospital environment. Constantly dealing with the learning curve of traveling nurses is time-consuming and often frustrating, as few have mastery and expertise.

Hospital human resources managers are also dealing with nursing staff burnout. Nurses are paid hourly, and they don't earn more by being more efficient and productive. There is no intrinsic incentive to do more surgeries. It makes more sense for them to take their time, and if anyone questions why things are taking so long, there are numerous places to point a finger.

However, the issue of staffing shortages can't be underestimated. Many physicians and nurses gave up their careers in healthcare during and after the COVID-19 pandemic. Some clinicians died. They were on the front lines, taking care of patients until the very end, putting their own lives in danger, especially when there were massive shortages of personal protective equipment.

Many healthcare workers, doing their best through the pandemic, changed their perspective on efficiency and what it meant to be good at their job. Maybe doing well means doing just enough so that you can come to work the next day. There is no glib or easy answer to staffing shortages. It's a multifaceted issue because it is dictated by a human factor.

We also must take into consideration the facility's hiring practices. They are experiencing the same erratic accounts receivable problems as our private practice. The hospitals need real expertise on the receivables and collections side of billing and collections, and I doubt they are as good as our practice. Hospital systems are larger and may not be agile enough to track the nuances in the same way we do in our practice. If the hospital doesn't have the revenue or margins it needs, the administrators will reflexively try to do more with less. From a human resources standpoint, it probably makes more sense for them to have more traveling nurses, with short-term contracts who don't qualify for benefits.

In his book *My Brother's Keeper,* author Nicholas Rosenlicht, M.D., notes that administrators in healthcare have increased significantly over the last 40 years relative to the number of clinicians. Today, a typical hospital has twice as many administrative staff as doctors and nurses. Why is that? What do all the administrators do? I'm sure I don't understand many of the dynamics. People are being hired to do a job, and they may be out of touch with how to be efficient in the model they're operating under.

I had moments of frustration in those days. Looking back, it seems I should have been more exasperated, but I was in the middle of a fight to get my operative cases done and to take care of my patients. I didn't have the benefit of hindsight.

CHAPTER 6

Building the Practice from the Ground Up

While operative cases define the technical side of an orthopedic surgery practice, managing a private doctor's office requires an MBA-level understanding of office management and business operations. And yet, few office managers hold that degree.

Shortly before Betty left the practice, we'd decided to expand our benefits package to implement a 401K plan for the staff. We were all new to the human resources system, and there was an issue with a double withdrawal. Naturally, Betty had access to the accounts, but when I asked what had happened, instead of simply saying, she tried to correct it without much luck. The amount, $40,000, was significant. That was when she chose to leave.

With Betty gone, we divided her role amongst the remaining staff. Initially, we tried looking for a replacement, with Michael helping us with the search, but in the end, we promoted a staff member to manage the business side and the physician assistant to take over clinical management.

We had moved away from a Venn diagram management style to something more linear, streamlined, and efficient, with clearly delineated areas of responsibility. I finally felt I had a handle on things. We were becoming a model of what a practice like ours should look like, but then the challenges we faced with USChoice began to escalate.

At the same time, in 2007, we decided to make a break with the practice we were renting our office space from to move to our own property. With our primary practice location in Springfield and a satellite in Bayonne, we started actively looking for a building that we would own. We looked in several locations, including Montclair, a more affluent community. But Bayonne turned out to be the best choice because it was close to Jersey City, where Marc was on call, and it was also closer to our home.

The space we found was probably the biggest selling point. The builder was known and respected. He had built out many medical office suites in a space that had been an American Legion Post. The building had parking, which was a huge bonus, and the builder had reserved the location we were looking at for a surgery center. Those plans had fallen through, and now, the builder was willing to custom-build to our needs.

The new office would become our primary, while Springfield, which we still rented, would become our satellite, where we would see patients one day a week. Then we also had to have that awkward conversation with the two older physicians who owned the Springfield building. Rather than a simple and casual conversation, we were called into a meeting where we had to share our vision and plans. They wished us the best of luck, but the feeling was very much that of grown-up kids leaving the paternal home.

But we were ready for the next chapter, as the practice evolved based on the changes in the insurance landscape.

Committing to establishing our practice in Bayonne meant I was adding another "small" item to my work plate. In addition to doing surgeries, seeing patients, and running the office, Marc and I were now in charge of creating an office space that was in alignment with our vision for our practice and that perfectly reflected our focus on patient care.

Our developer was in his late 80s or early 90s. His partner, the primary general contractor, was Nick Louvrous, who had already completed four of the six medical office spaces in the building. After our initial meeting, when he realized we were serious about purchasing the remaining space, he started taking us to a local diner every two weeks or so to talk about our vision.

Essentially, Nick was reversing the role I'd played with Betty, and he did it well.

Marc, Nick, and I talked about the space and our requirements for the practice. Nick thoroughly explained his process, including laying tiles and carpeting, and installing the plumbing, all to our specifications. He also introduced us to his architect. And somewhere along the way, we successfully negotiated the built-to-suit purchase price. After we sealed the deal, we'd still find ourselves at a diner or in the under-construction office space, looking at tile selections, paint colors, and carpet samples. I was particular about what I wanted, and justifiably, I believe. The patient experience was always my prime consideration, and I was willing to go to considerable trouble to make sure it was the best it could be.

We drove to a wholesaler in an industrial New Jersey commercial strip to pick out cabinets for each of the five examination rooms and the employee break room. I was especially particular about the front office counter that patients inevitably leaned on when talking to the staff. I'd noticed that in the other doctor's offices Nick had built, the counters were wobbly. "You can't give us what you gave them," I said.

I consulted the contractor who had done work in our kitchen at home the year before and had sourced the perfect countertop. I also insisted that its support had to be sturdy. Eighteen years later, our counter at the reception area still doesn't wobble.

The X-ray machine in our office was another huge investment, not only in money, but in time and attention. In 2006–2007, most hospitals and doctors' offices were switching to digital X-rays. We did our due diligence, even driving to Princeton to consider our X-ray options. Because it was a newer technology at the time, it was expensive. The system we settled on cost almost $400,000. Aside from the cost, the main issue now was getting the huge machine and accompanying electrical connections into our space. We gave the X-ray distribution firm our architectural renderings. The X-ray suite had to have a lead layer in the wall along with the sheet rock. Due to construction limitations, once the door was installed, its location was fixed.

At the eleventh hour, after they had already approved the architect's rendering, the X-ray firm told us the door to the suite was in the wrong place, and they wouldn't be able to move the X-ray machine into the room.

Not good.

"We have to make it work," we said. "We ran this by you. The walls are where they are." In the end, there was only one solution: they had to find a way to move the door without destroying the lead in the walls. They did it successfully, but the room was never ideal.

Most of our X-rays do not require the patient to lie down. But when they do, when taking a pelvis or spine X-ray, for instance, the patient must be supine[1] on the table, and we have always had challenges getting our beautiful, plexiglass X-ray table in and out of the X-ray room, due to its length and the lack of vendor forethought in creating the suite. The X-ray table is a constant reminder of the fact that our needs were not heard the first time.

In September 2007, the office space was completed at last, right down to our choice of toilets and sinks for the washrooms. An

---

[1] Lying face upwards.

important feature of the office was wide, handicapped accessible hallways, so patients could be easily pushed in on a stretcher or enter the exam room in a wheelchair, with their leg fully extended if necessary. We could have maximized the space and put in an additional examination room, but it really was all about the patients. Wider hallways and larger examination rooms made more sense to us.

Building our office was a lot of work. But we were optimistic and excited. We were creating our own practice, from the ground up, and we believed that once we had it built out and turned our focus to developing the expertise we needed to run it efficiently, we would no longer have to worry about erratic reimbursements from the private insurance companies, and our financial pressures would disappear.

To our surprise, as our expertise increased, our reimbursements were heading in the opposite direction, getting lower and lower, with the timing of repayment stretching out longer and longer.

Hmmm...

At that time, we developed a relationship with a local university, Rutgers Business School, offering internships to their undergraduate students and, a couple of times, to master's students. At our practice, the interns received excellent exposure to medical billing, accounting, and collections. We particularly liked one or two and asked them if they would like to stay on, develop experience, and rise to the position of office manager or business manager. After experiencing what we had to go through, they were smart enough to say, "This has been a great experience. I really like you, but I'm going to work for an accounting firm or on the insurance side of healthcare."

They appreciated the lack of politics in our practice, but the job couldn't offer the quality of job satisfaction they were looking for. No matter how hard they worked, the benefits didn't balance out the frustrations, and the recurrent challenges continued to escalate. No matter how good our business staff were at their jobs, they still observed significant reductions in reimbursements for office hours, surgeries, and injections while the timeframe for accounts receivable increased. In 2007, if office hours were busy, the revenue would be enough to cover payroll and our office expenses. Surgeries were not essential to our bottom line. But with the passing of each year, we found ourselves relying more and more heavily on surgical revenues.

It's far easier to identify the problems looking back with 20 years of gained wisdom. But at the time, Marc and I and the members of our staff were firmly focused on our patients, making sure we were taking proper care of them. Their successes were our rewards. We concentrated on keeping up with our charts and documentation and getting our surgeries done.

However, all along the way, we were fighting with the private insurance companies. Where we hoped they would have been our healthcare partners, they were behaving more like our adversaries, and language was one of their weapons.

"Prior authorization" was a concept we increasingly had to deal with. And let me make a very important note here: prior authorization is in no way a guarantee of payment. You need prior authorization to get paid, but having it doesn't mean you will.

Prior authorization is a strategy employed by the insurance companies to enforce utilization management, which, as I said previously, I call utilization minimization, not management. In other words, what is the least the insurer can get away with doing for any given patient? Prior authorization essentially enforces an arbitrary waiting period. We must request authorization in advance to get a procedure done. Insurers make a big deal of our request, inspecting every facet, making sure we cross our t's and dot our i's, and clear any other hurdle they place in front of us in order to provide our patient with the care they need.

We need prior authorization to perform an MRI. Until recently, we didn't need it to do a CT scan. Now we do. Some insurers require prior authorization for pain medication like OxyContin after extensive surgery, like a total joint replacement. A pharmacy will not fill the prescription under the insurance company plan unless the prior authorization is on record. The patient could pay for it out of pocket if necessary. What we are seeing often now, however, is the pharmacy waiting to get authorization before obtaining the medication from their formulary. Even pharmacies are enforcing a waiting period.

Here's another phrase: "Current Procedural Terminology" (CPT). Everything we do is represented by a CPT code. The insurance company takes that code and may decide it needs more information from the patient's chart or medical history. What is fascinating to me is that when we request the fee schedule, the amount we are to be paid for the most commonly billed codes, we rarely receive a timely response, if we receive a response at all. Regarding our prior authorizations, someone at the insurance company reviews the information, compares it with the CPT code, and makes a decision. We began to find that the decision could take as long as four days or more.

Was I getting frustrated?

We were jumping through all the payors' hoops to provide clinical information to get prior authorization, which, honestly, appears to be a tool to keep us from doing what we are bound to do by the Hippocratic Oath.

Marc and I learned about a breast surgeon in Texas who posted a video online, in which she shared her experience of being literally called out of the operating room to speak with a representative from her patient's insurance company. She was told it was an "emergency regarding the breast cancer patient she had on the table." The person placing the call from the insurance company did not know the patient had breast cancer. And yet, they asked the question, "Is this procedure medically necessary?"

The doctor also posted on her Instagram account that they rescinded the authorization and that the insurance company refused to pay for the patient's surgery.

Here are the facts: It was breast cancer. Surgery was necessary, not optional.

Another fact: This is what is happening.

We also saw a news story on television entitled "The Cost of Denial," where prior authorization for a child's ear reconstruction surgery was granted minutes before she entered the operating room.

Doctors are being called out of the operating room. Marc and I never had that experience, but it all comes back to prior authorization, and more and more, it entails multiple reviews.

For that Texas surgeon to enter the operating room with her patient, she had to have had prior authorization. We know that, but somehow, a review process took place, and the insurer wanted a take-back of the authorization.

Utilization management is just another phrase in the language war insurance companies are waging. They want to deter patients from having unnecessary care and to minimize the use of necessary care. I see it as a game of chicken: "I dare you! Who's going to flinch first?"

That's where we are in our practice. We've always been committed to our patients. If we recommend a procedure, we wholeheartedly believe it is necessary, and we will be persistent in getting authorization. If it's denied, we will appeal and request a peer review from another orthopedic surgeon. Even then, it's not easy.

A patient presented to our local medical center with a locked knee, meaning he could not bend it further or straighten it fully. Nine times out of ten, that's what's called a bucket handle meniscus tear, meaning there is a piece of meniscus that has flipped up into the joint and is preventing motion of the knee. With local anesthesia and manipulation, they can reduce the tear. The patient had an MRI, but the radiologist did not read the bucket-handle meniscus tear. It read something like "abnormal meniscus" but did not explicitly state "meniscus tear." The patient also had an anterior cruciate ligament (ACL) tear.

When we read the MRI in our practice, it was clear there was a bucket handle meniscus tear. The diagnosis indicated surgery. After our prior authorization request was denied, we proceeded to request a peer review from the insurer. That particular orthopedic surgeon said, "You have approval for the ACL tear, but the radiologist did not read the meniscus tear, so you have two options. One, you can ask them to revise their report."

That was not an option because it would take time, and surgery was scheduled for the next day.

The other option, he gave us: "You can remove the meniscus tear from the prior authorization for the surgery."

We could do that, but it would also mean we would not be paid for the work we did on the meniscus.

He went on to say that he could not give us authorization for the ACL reconstruction unless we agreed to remove the meniscus tear from the prior authorization. He was asking us to resubmit a request for authorization to encompass only the ACL reconstruction, not the meniscus repair that was required. But he was also an orthopedic surgeon, so he knew that not getting the meniscus repaired could predispose the patient to arthritis in the future. In another scenario, his knee might be locked. The surgeon was entirely aware of that, just as he was aware that the clinical request we had made was required.

"This is not a denial," he said. "This is just the absence of a prior authorization."

And all of this was just to get us into the operating room. It was not a guarantee of payment. You would think that after overcoming all these hurdles and doing exactly what we said we would do, payment would be automatic.

Not so. When we submitted our claim, we started from scratch.

We did the full surgery, putting in the claim for both the ACL reconstruction and the meniscus repair. And it wasn't just our practice that had to fight for reimbursement; the hospital did too. And that is the objective of the insurance companies: to pay for as little of the patient's care as possible. If it were truly about the patient, I wouldn't be writing this book.

We were still learning, but as we did, we gathered more ammunition. We instructed the staff about what questions they would have to answer when requesting prior authorization for any procedures, including MRIs. As orthopedic surgeons, we made several prior authorization requests for imaging each day. We created three-ring binders of a hundred pages each, listing all the diagnoses and detailing exactly what to say and what to write to get prior authorization for each body part. Our office manager handed one of these binders to each staff member. They couldn't simply look at a patient's chart; they had to know exactly what the insurer was looking for, specific to the CPT code. They had to be able to enumerate every stage of conservative treatment, including anti-inflammatory medicine or physical therapy. Every step had to be documented.

Of course, handling the massive amounts of paperwork also required more people to be able to manage it, so we had to hire more staff. The same is true for hospitals, and that may, in part at least, answer Nicholas Rosenlicht's question of why there has been a dramatic rise in administrative positions in the healthcare field.

We cross-train our staff because we can't afford to have them do just one thing. Our staff must be able to get prior authorizations while also checking in patients, talking to insurance companies, filling in for each other, and getting a peer review done. And this is the patient care side, not billing and collections. They also have to know how to get ancillary studies done for conditions like carpal tunnel syndrome because those were also reports we needed to get prior authorization.

We had to jump through hoops to get a prior authorization for an MRI, which we needed to get a prior authorization to do surgery. Hoops within hoops. In the case of our young patient with the bucket handle meniscus tear, I had to call the radiologist and ask him to rewrite his report to include it as part of his injury.

Again, looking back, it's easy to see the issues, but at the time, we just had our heads down, doing what we had to do. We weren't analyzing the system; we were caring for our patients. We didn't ask why, and we couldn't opt out of the system. If we fought it, we were never going to win. We simply accepted every new rule and requirement for prior authorization.

We adapted. We trained our staff. We continued to expand our catalogue of capabilities to meet every new demand. For us, it was a question of one foot in front of the other as we plodded along.

However, no matter what we did, we saw fewer payments from the insurance companies and more and more money from the patients in terms of copays and deductibles. At the same time, payment from the insurers was stretching from 30 days to 60, 90, and even 120 days.

Our frustration was mostly on behalf of our patients. Our goal was to get them the surgery, therapy, and treatment they needed. The insurance companies were actively trying to prevent us from doing that. Our priority was to make enough money to keep the practice solvent so that we could continue to take care of our patients. When we had to start digging into our savings to keep the doors open, we started taking a hard look at what was going on.

We are bound by the Hippocratic Oath. The physicians providing prior authorization through insurance companies are not. As soon as we begin to train as doctors, we are taught to compartmentalize our emotions. In a life and death situation, you have to be able to step outside yourself and step into being the doctor. You must focus, sift, filter, and bring someone from the edge of death back to life. It requires a certain presence. Bringing that into this situation, I operate as a doctor trying to make the best of a terrible situation, while feeling that other doctors, employed by insurers, have left my patients and me to the whim of the insurance company's arbitrary policies. I've been trained to deal with terrible circumstances, so I keep doing what I do.

In this case, terrible is the increasing death-grip of the insurance industry on the healthcare profession.

CHAPTER 7

Puzzle Pieces that Form an Invisible Hand

While Marc and I were still wholeheartedly patient-focused, we had also become acutely aware of the environment we were operating in, which required us to develop increased agility and expertise in making real-time adaptations and decisions, including those related to our billing and collections. One consideration that arose almost annually was, "Should we outsource these operations?" Many doctors in our community were, and it made sense–they wanted to focus on healthcare, not on the complicated details of dealing with insurance companies. To have more resources to offer their patients, they opted to hire a company or collections specialist who had the expertise to handle their medical practice's billing and collections.

Marc and I were approached at least once a quarter by companies or "experts" who wanted to take on our accounts receivable billings and collections. Some were retired practice managers or billers who offered to work with us as consultants. The offers were always tempting, but I had a couple of reservations. First, their offers felt too good to be true.

Ours was a solo practice, and if our billing specialist's clientele included larger practices or organizations, would they put more focus on the larger organization's billing and collections rather than ours? Would we be a small fish in a large medical collections pond and therefore not receive the detailed attention we so desperately required?

Also, medical accounts receivable is nuanced. Billing for an internal medicine practice is very different from billing for a general surgery or an orthopedic surgery practice. Everything we do in medicine is quantified by the Current Procedural Terminology (CPT) code, a national quantification of the work that we do. Additionally, the regulations surrounding the use of these codes are constantly changing. For example, private insurance companies may adopt Medicare guidelines. Patients might not be under Medicare, but when the government establishes a new guideline for Medicare, it will eventually become the industry standard. We must be vigilant and ever aware of the release of new guidelines, which may be issued annually, but could also be issued at any time. Would the collections "specialist" understand the nuances of the coding guidelines for orthopedic surgery?

That wasn't my only concern. I also worried about the loss of autonomy and control. When we dealt with billing our accounts receivable, we did so in a timely fashion with no delays. We escalated our attention to detail in alignment with the accounts receivable (AR) challenges, so that we were running reports weekly, and sometimes every other day. We understood exactly, at any given time, which insurer's claims were being paid, and which were not, as well as which claims were being rejected due to recent changes in Medicare or private insurance guidelines. We also knew which insurers had idiosyncratic requirements we had to meet.

Regarding idiosyncrasies, orthopedic surgery has two lateralities; in other words, each patient has two upper and two lower extremities. If a patient had issues with both shoulders, then, depending on the insurer, we might have to bill them differently. Bilaterality means something different to Cigna than it does to Medicare or UnitedHealthcare. Our billing specialists had to know those details. About outsourcing, naturally, I was concerned about not having the ability to oversee the biller or collector, to understand in real-time that they operated with that level of detail.

We have always been a small, private practice. Every case matters to us, and after giving it careful thought, each time we were approached, we would reassess our alternatives, and each time we ultimately chose not to outsource our billings and collections, continuing to assume the responsibility to manage both the clinical and business side of our practice. There was too much at stake to risk the consequences of entrusting our finances to an outside party.

Like most healthcare organizations in the last decade, even before the COVID-19 pandemic, we also continue to cope with staffing shortages. Certainly, this became a far more apparent problem when COVID-19 exploded the state of healthcare onto the global stage. Marc and I only wanted staff who had the educational background and personality traits that would equip them to contribute positively to the practice for years to come. Often this requires months-long searches for the right people who would be the face of the practice at our front desk and who have the fortitude as well as the attention to detail necessary to support the quality of care we are determined to offer. Hiring is a daunting task.

Unfortunately, over time, we frequently witnessed genuinely nice people becoming callous, primarily because they were overwhelmed with the challenge of looking after the needs of our patients while trying to communicate with them empathetically. Just like the interns we hired from Rutgers School of Business, the staff we hoped would become permanent confessed that our work was too draining.

Gabby, our red-haired, 20-something front desk manager, confessed, "I'd rather work at a hospital where I can focus on only one set of tasks. I don't know how you do it, Doctor Urquhart. It's just so hard here, in private practice. You and your husband are so nice, but I don't want to be *this* challenged every day."

Staff who left the office practice often shared that they felt overwhelmed by the cross-training and overburdened by working in an environment where they were expected to know more than just their primary duties.

By this time, I had acquired enough expertise in managing erratic accounts receivable that I could unequivocally say "yes" to a friend who asked me to participate as an instructor in a Mastery Summit for Entrepreneurs, primarily because I believe every entrepreneur has an obligation to be strategic as they look at the timing of their revenues.

I made three key points:
1. Through 25 years in the practice of medicine, I have learned how to operate in an industry that is adversarial to my ultimate goal of providing quality, efficient patient care.
2. I've acquired specific insights into the entrepreneurial aspects of my journey that are applicable across multiple sectors, not just healthcare.
3. My niche: I have developed tools for keeping one's business afloat; a multistep system to overcome erratic accounts receivable.

The first point was important for us personally. We had to apply our diagnostic skills to determine who or what our adversary was, day in and day out. We had to understand that the insurance companies were, to put it bluntly, our enemy.

Instead of acting as a partner in patient care, the private insurers were examining our claims using an arbitrary set of criteria and taking every opportunity to routinely deny them. How accurately we are billing is not the criterion they measure, because even with claim-scrubbing software in place, they still deny about a quarter of the cases we submit. So, we have no choice but to resubmit. Over time, based on the patterns I was seeing, I developed a theory about the denials. I have no proof, but all my anecdotal evidence points to many private insurers using AI to assess whether we are paying attention to our billing and collections.

If our staff got behind by a couple of weeks, not closely eyeing the reports, and not calling private insurers to follow up on the claims, we would see a precipitous increase in the number of cases that were rejected.

Speaking at the entrepreneurial mastery summit via a virtual format, I expounded on the techniques any business adversary may use to withhold accounts receivable. During this process, as I began writing it down, I realized how much valuable and generally relevant knowledge I had accumulated.

In our practice, we focused on cross-training, remaining agile, and continuing to stay up to date on the latest tactics employed to avoid fully reimbursing us for our work.

Every day, Marc and I find ourselves compensating for the fact that our accounts receivable are inconsistent. We never know if we will receive payment in 30, 60, 90, or 120 days. Running a business with that kind of uncertainty is always a challenge.

A byproduct of all this was a toxic work environment, not just in our practice, but throughout healthcare. Our staff felt overburdened, even though we worked hard to ensure they were gone by 6 p.m. We didn't ask them to take work home or to stay late. But the intensity of dealing with patients while also making sure we dotted every "i" and crossed every "t" was debilitating for a lot of people.

Healthcare staff work in an unforgiving environment. As a doctor and a healer, you must be near-perfect. You cannot make mistakes. Then, because of the tight margins, we cannot make mistakes on the business side either. The insurance information must be entered accurately. The communication with patients must be precise. Patients will be upset if you're not communicating fully and accurately.

There is zero margin for error, and that stress can create a toxic environment in every aspect of healthcare.

Marc frequently takes orthopedic trauma calls at a level two trauma center. Most orthopedic surgeries are not life-threatening, but if someone has been in an accident and is helicoptered in, Marc is often the go-to surgeon. One evening, he had just finished taking care of an injury and, at about 2 a.m., prepared to do another surgery on a nurse from California who had been visiting a family member in New Jersey when she injured her wrist in a fall.

When the nurse heard that Marc was trained in a hand fellowship and was on call that night, she asked to have her surgery done before flying back home in a few days. There was absolutely no reason not to do it. She was a nurse, well-insured, and with an injury the surgeon on call could take care of easily.

Marc said, "Yes. Sure. Send her up! We'll take care of this."

A happy side-effect was that this would also build the reputation of the institution through word of mouth.

Before performing the surgery, Marc had to speak to the anesthesiologist on call to get their approval. The patient hadn't eaten. She was ready. The anesthesiologist asked, "Is it an emergency?"

"It's a wrist fracture," Marc said. "It is certainly urgent, and the wrist is broken with a complex fracture pattern that must be treated operatively. Is it life or death? No. But it is urgent. She's a nurse. She needs to have the surgery. If you want me to use the words, 'It's an emergency,' all right, I'll use those words. But it's not life or death."

The anesthesiologist nodded. "All right. We'll do the case."

They rolled the patient's stretcher up to the operating room. A representative of the company that supplied the implant for the wrist fracture happened to be in the hallway just out of the line of sight of the entrance to the operating room. As Marc was about to step through the doors, the certified nurse anesthetist, who worked with the anesthesiologist, stepped in front of him, blocking him from entering. Pointing his finger at Marc, he said, "You're a bully. You always do this. You're always trying to make us do these cases. I don't understand why you're like this."

Marc is a six-foot-four African American. The nurse anesthetist was a short white guy. It was the middle of the night, and Marc could have decided not to be tolerant of the rude, derogatory, and unprofessional behavior. And though neither man knew, the incident was witnessed by the sales representative standing in the corridor.

Marc simply walked away, and although he reported the incident to the disciplinary committee, no disciplinary measure was ever enacted, nor did he receive a response.

I believe that incident was the definition of a toxic work environment.

That toxicity has multiple sources. It's not just about one nurse anesthetist in one hospital. Health insurers are also making our job of caring for patients more difficult.

I referred earlier to the Cigna CEO quoted in the *Intelligencer* article as saying they "needed to execute a few hostages." Well, we, too, have been dropped by insurers. We were unilaterally dismissed from UnitedHealthcare's panel without explanation. When we asked why, they told us they had sent forms to our office, which we had not completed. However, no one in our office had received those forms. And in prior years, we had never received such a request.

As Ron Howrigon described, terminating doctors whose patients needed the most. Prior to termination, we were one of the few practices in our area affiliated with UnitedHealthcare. When we were dropped, we did some sleuthing and learned that our patients were already paying out-of-pocket for most of their care as a copay. We offered those patients with that insurer to come to our office anyway and just pay what they would have paid to the insurer.

My frustration was mounting.

CHAPTER 8

Revisiting the Anatomy of The Invisible Hand

I've made the case that the free market forces of healthcare in the United States have created a pivotal financial role for commercial insurance companies to play in our lives, but I also want to look at the big picture. If insurers are doing their best to retain premiums, then what is the end result for patients, the consumers of healthcare? In other words, how are we performing with our current system of health in the United States? Can we afford the care we need at every stage in our lives?

Certainly, we now understand the insurers are doing their best to guard the threshold of healthcare with a decisive palm forward, so they do not have to pay. Instead of expensive imaging studies and surgeries, they're cutting the care patients can receive using prior authorizations and utilization management strategies. This is not just a matter of occasional denials; 41% of healthcare providers now report that at least 1 in 10 claims are denied, reflecting a widespread and growing barrier that delays necessary care and shifts financial burdens unfairly onto patients and providers alike.[1] If this trend continues unchecked, the

---

[1] National Planning Cycles, "Healthcare claim denial statistics: State of Claims Report 2025" https://nationalplanningcycles.org/healthcare-claim-denial-statistics-state-of-claims-report-2025/

consequences will only deepen the crisis of access and affordability. Because these tools are so effective, causing three quarters of patients to abandon their treatment plans, insurance companies' hands are effectively raising the palm, and placing providers and patients into a holding pattern.

But how are we going to get well in this system where the invisible hand is snapped up in warning, staying our entry into utilization of healthcare services, withholding from patients the services our collective insurance premiums pay for, with the message, "You cannot afford to be healthy. Because your insurance is not going to pay."

I plunged into the existing research and literature, piecing together insights that shed light on these pressing financial constraints. Each article I read, or piece of data I studied, led to the same conclusion: Americans' healthcare spending is going up while patient health outcomes are going down.

Ten million working-age Americans now live on a financial knife's edge, hit with medical bills that swallow more than 5% of their income year after year. For a typical family earning $84,370 in 2022, that means paying roughly $5,950 annually just for care. Layered on top of premiums, those bills consume at least 14–15% of their income, about the same share they spend to keep a roof over their heads; so nearly two-thirds of their paychecks vanish into housing and healthcare before they can think about anything else. And the people bearing this burden are not statistical abstractions: they are disproportionately older, earning less, and living with more chronic illness, punished financially precisely because they are sicker and poorer.[2]

From a national perspective, the Kaiser Family Foundation's Health System Tracker put the American situation succinctly, noting that U.S. health spending (National Health Expenditures, or NHE) totaled $74.1

---

[2] Third Way. (2022). *Takeaways*. In *Chronic care cost-cap* (report summary). Retrieved August 29, 2025, from https://www.jstor.org/stable/resrep46920

billion in 1970. However, by 2000, health expenditures had reached about $1.4 trillion, and in 2023, the amount spent on health in America more than tripled to $4.9 trillion.[3] (Total health expenditures include not only the amount spent on healthcare and related activities, but also the administration of insurance, health research, and public health from both public and private funds.)

U.S. Health Expenditure Over Time

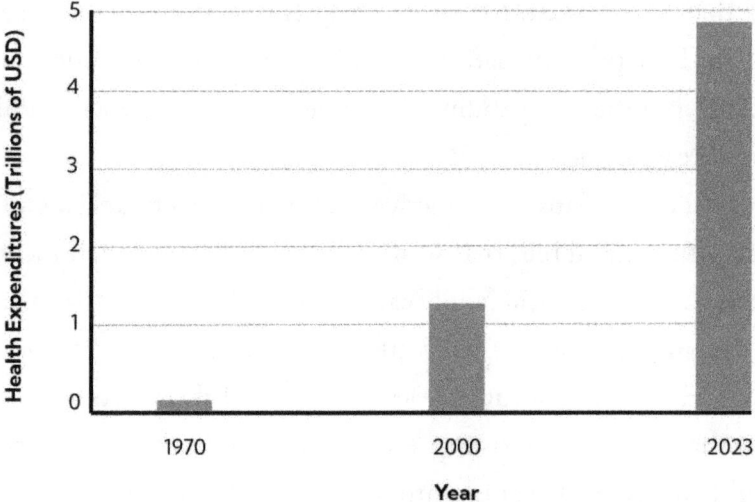

In a healthcare system where total expenditures soar into the stratospheric trillions, breaking those numbers down into a per capita context offers a clearer, more tangible perspective. By translating the vast national spending into individual terms, we see the true scale of the

---

[3] McGough, M., Wager, E., Winger, A., Panchal, N., & Cotter, L. (2024, December 20). How has U.S. spending on healthcare changed over time? *Peterson-KFF Health System Tracker*. Retrieved from https://www.kff.org/health-costs/chart-collection/u-s-spending-healthcare-changed-time/

financial burden each person carries, revealing the stark reality behind the statistics and why reform is not just necessary, but urgent.

Breaking that into numbers we can understand, on a per capita basis, health spending has increased in the last five decades from $353 per year in 1970 to $14,570 per year in 2023. America's healthcare system drains trillions each year, but what does that staggering number really mean for each individual? Accounting for inflation in 2023 dollars, the per-person cost increased from $2,151 in 1970 to $14,570 in 2023.[4]

Per Capita U.S. Health Spending: 1970 vs. 2023

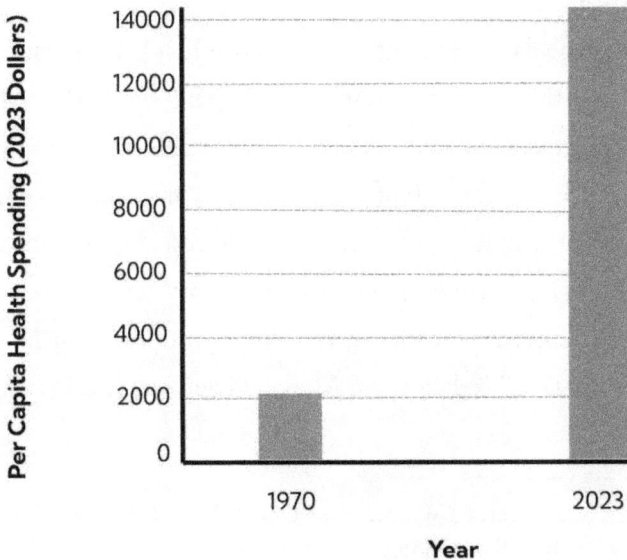

[4] McGough, M., Wager, E., Winger, A., Panchal, N., & Cotter, L. (2024, December 20). How has U.S. spending on healthcare changed over time? *Peterson-KFF Health System Tracker*. Retrieved from https://www.kff.org/health-costs/chart-collection/u-s-spending-healthcare-changed-time/

Healthcare continues to consume an ever-growing portion of the economy, reaching a staggering 19.5% of the gross domestic product (GDP) in 2020, nearly one-fifth of all economic activity. This immense share underscores the magnitude of healthcare's impact on both the national budget and everyday lives. Since 2022, health spending has represented a similar share of the economy as it did prior to the COVID-19 pandemic. Third-party private health insurance accounted for the largest share of national spending on health consumption expenditures in 2023 (30.1%). Proving my point, powerful and unyielding, third-party private health insurance dominates national health spending, again, claiming one-third in 2023, exerting immense influence over the lives of millions and shaping the relentless financial pressures that define today's healthcare crisis.

Looking at the data from another lens, not just health insurance, we find public health programs managed in part by CMS, Medicare, Medicaid, and the Children's Health Insurance Program (CHIP), accounted for 43.0%, nearly half, of all health consumption spending.[5] Interestingly, although Medicare and Medicaid spending have increased, studies have shown that orthopedic physician reimbursement for revision total knee replacements has not kept up with inflation since 2002.[6] So, Centers for Medicare and Medicaid Services (CMS) is spending

---

[5] McGough, M., Wager, E., Winger, A., Panchal, N., & Cotter, L. (2024, December 20). How has U.S. spending on healthcare changed over time? *Peterson–KFF Health System Tracker*. Retrieved from https://www.kff.org/health-costs/chart-collection/u-s-spending-healthcare-changed-time/

[6] Jella, Tarun K. MPH1; Acuña, Alexander J. BS1; Samuel, Linsen T. MD, MBA1; Schwarzkopf, Ran MD, MSc2; Fehring, Thomas K. MD3; Kamath, Atul F. MD1,a. Medicare Physician Fee Reimbursement for Revision Total Knee Arthroplasty Has Not Kept Up with Inflation from 2002 to 2019. The Journal of Bone and Joint Surgery 103(9):p 778-785, May 5, 2021. | DOI: 10.2106/JBJS.20.01034

more but paying doctors less. The same is true for revision of hip replacements.[7] These two studies conclude that there is a "consistent devaluation" of revision hip and knee replacement procedures. The authors also infer that a continuation of this trend, paying doctors less by not keeping pace with inflation, could create disincentives and limit patient access to care. And this is just one example, in orthopedic surgery.

The Peter G. Peterson Foundation's last word on the subject is this:

While the United States spends more on healthcare than any other high-income country, the nation often performs worse on measures of health and healthcare. Not only is the U.S. the only high-income OECD country we studied that does not have universal health coverage, a substantial percentage of residents lack health coverage. Its insurance-financed health structure, focused on prior authorizations and other gatekeeping measures, seems designed to discourage people from using healthcare services.[8]

Behind all the calculations and statistics are real people with real stories. For America, the first step to improvement is ensuring that everyone has access to affordable care. US Senator Bernie Sanders is often quoted as presenting the view, "Healthcare is a human right and not a privilege. The function of a rational healthcare system is not to make billions in profits for insurance companies and the pharmaceutical industry, but to provide quality care for all."

---

[7] Wang R, Li X, Gu X, Cai Q, Wang Y, Yi ZM, Chen LC. The impact of China's zero markup drug policy on drug costs for managing Parkinson's disease and its complications: an interrupted time series analysis. Front Public Health. 2023 May 9;11:1159119. doi: 10.3389/fpubh.2023.1159119. PMID: 37228740; PMCID: PMC10203530.

[8] Third Way. (2022). *Chronic care cost cap* [Report]. Retrieved August 29, 2025, from https://www.thirdway.org/report/chronic-care-cost-cap

Third Way tells the story of Stacey Armato, a 41-year-old mother of three living in Hermosa Beach, California. Her six-year-old son with cystic fibrosis takes about a dozen medications, costing thousands of dollars. The Armato's insurance limits the annual benefit to Stacey's son to $6,000 a year. The high out-of-pocket costs that the Armato's shoulder is not rare. Their expenses for pulmonary care for their young child exceed 7% of the family's income, and to properly care for their child, the Armatos must pay this amount year after year.[9]

Similar to the Armatos, families with lower incomes face a greater financial burden from high out-of-pocket costs. Twelve percent of families with persistent high costs and low incomes qualify federally for free coverage through Medicaid, but they may not be enrolled, or they may live in one of the 12 states that have not expanded Medicaid to include them.

Additionally, people with more chronic conditions face higher out-of-pocket costs, and the risk increases with the number of chronic conditions people have. For example, the National Council on Aging reported the dilemma an elderly gentleman named Robert faces daily. A 75-year-old who has had two heart attacks must decide between paying for heart medications and basic utility bills, illustrating the tradeoff between life-sustaining care and essential living expenses. Robert's fate, like millions of others, is in the hands of a complex coverage system.[10]

The American Medical Association published its latest findings in April 2025, reflecting the findings of every research site I examined. The

---

[9] Wolfson, B. J. (2021, November 17). *Your out-of-pocket healthcare costs need not be a mystery*. Kaiser Health News. Retrieved August 29, 2025, from https://www.pasadenanow.com/weekendr/your-out-of-pocket-health-care-costs-needArmatos-not-be-a-mystery/

[10] CBS Interactive. (n.d.). What we know about Luigi Mangione, suspect charged in UnitedHealthcare CEO's killing. CBS News. https://www.cbsnews.com/news/luigi-mangione-healthcare-ceo-shooting-what-we-know/

National Health Expenditures (NHE) fact sheet breaks the summary down neatly:

Historical NHE, 2023

- NHE grew 7.5% to $4.9 trillion in 2023, or $14,570 per person, and accounted for 17.6% of Gross Domestic Product (GDP).
- Medicare spending grew 8.1% to $1,029.8 billion in 2023, or 21% of total NHE.
- Medicaid spending grew 7.9% to $871.7 billion in 2023, or 18% of total NHE.
- Private health insurance spending grew 11.5% to $1,464.6 billion in 2023, or 30% of total NHE.
- Out-of-pocket spending grew 7.2% to $505.7 billion in 2023, or 10% of total NHE.
- Other Third-Party Payers and Programs and Public Health Activity spending declined 3.1% in 2023 to $563.4 billion, or 12% of total NHE.
- Hospital expenditures grew 10.4% to $1,519.7 billion in 2023, faster than the 3.2% growth in 2022.
- Physician and clinical services expenditures grew 7.4% to $978.0 billion in 2023, faster growth than the 4.6% in 2022
- Prescription drug spending increased 11.4% to $449.7 billion in 2023, faster than the 7.8 % growth in 2022.
- The largest shares of total health spending were sponsored by the federal government (32%) and households (27%). The private business share of health spending accounted for 18% of total healthcare spending, state and local governments accounted for 16%, and other private revenues accounted for 7%.[11]

---

[11] Centers for Medicare & Medicaid Services. (2024, November). *Historical national health expenditures, 2023*. CMS. Retrieved August 29, 2025, from

$4.9 Trillion
Total NHE ↑ 7.5%
($14,570/person, 17.6% GDP)

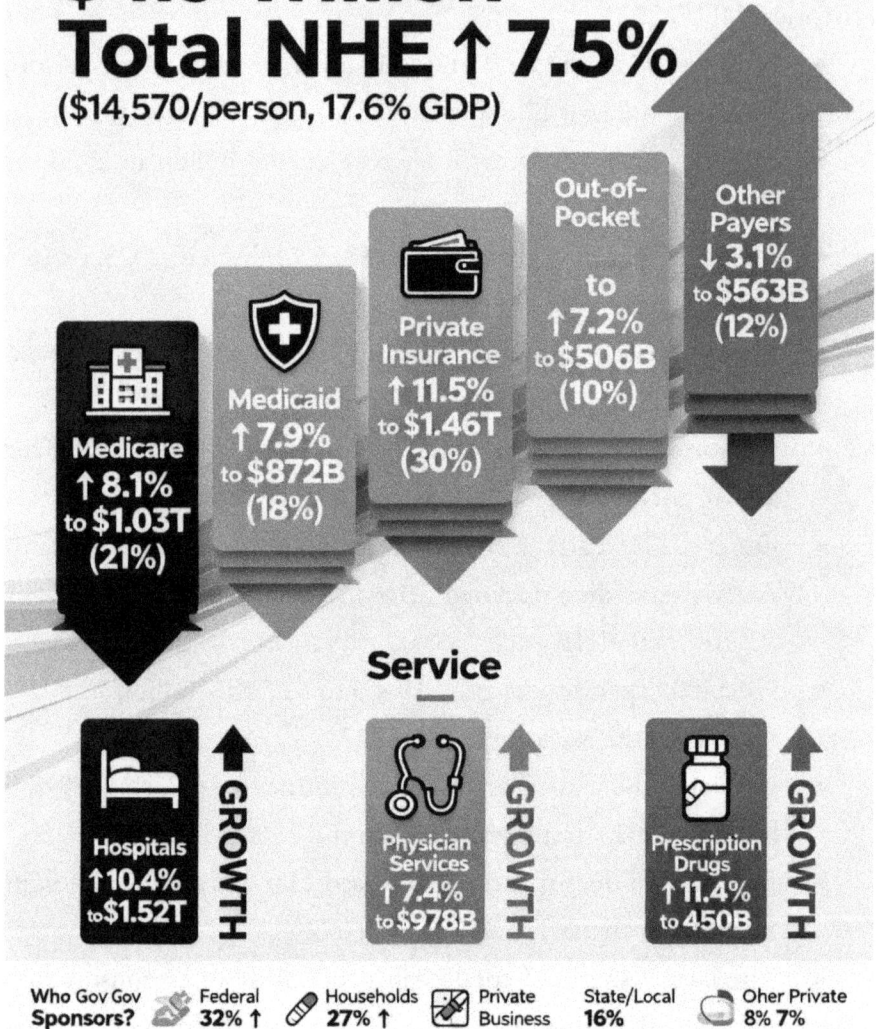

Medicare
↑ 8.1%
to $1.03T
(21%)

Medicaid
↑ 7.9%
to $872B
(18%)

Private Insurance
↑ 11.5%
to $1.46T
(30%)

Out-of-Pocket
to ↑ 7.2%
to $506B
(10%)

Other Payers
↓ 3.1%
to $563B
(12%)

Service

Hospitals
↑ 10.4%
to $1.52T

GROWTH

Physician Services
↑ 7.4%
to $978B

GROWTH

Prescription Drugs
↑ 11.4%
to 450B

GROWTH

Who Gov Gov Sponsors?	Federal 32% ↑	Households 27% ↑	Private Business	State/Local 16%	Oher Private 8% 7%

Projections for the next 10 years are not optimistic. The price of healthcare will also increase, but will the patient's purchasing power? The

---

https://www.cms.gov/data-research/statistics-trends-and-reports/national-health-expenditure-data/nhe-fact-sheet government expects NHE growth to outpace GDP growth, resulting in even more lop-sided spending on healthcare. The next 10 years could bring steep rises in healthcare spending. The government warns that healthcare costs will outstrip economic growth, pushing families and the nation into even deeper financial strain. Already, more and more patients are having difficulty keeping up with expensive insurance premiums and prescription drugs.

We hear stories of many families who, like Robert, are making choices between healthcare and paying the rent. The forecast doesn't show an improvement in this particular state of affairs.

In 2020, Americans 65 and older spent an average of $22,356 each on personal healthcare, over five times what is spent on a child ($4,217) and nearly two and a half times the spending on a working-age adult ($9,154). For many seniors, that level of spending devours a massive share of their fixed or limited income.[12]

The amount the United States spends on healthcare is tremendous. But how does it compare to other countries? As I noted, we spend about $14,570 per person, and by comparison, the average cost of healthcare per person in other wealthy countries is less than half what Americans spend. The Commonwealth Fund, a private, American-based foundation focused on improving the U.S. healthcare system, says that while we are accelerating spending, we are seeing worsening outcomes. It notes that in all countries, health spending as a share of the overall economy has been steadily increasing since the 1980s, but in 2021, the U.S. spent 17.8% of gross domestic product (GDP) on healthcare, nearly

---

[12] Centers for Medicare & Medicaid Services. (2024). *National Health Expenditure (NHE) fact sheet: Per person personal healthcare spending by age group*. Retrieved August 29, 2025, from https://www.cms.gov/data-research/statistics-trends-and-reports/national-health-expenditure-data/nhe-fact-sheet

twice as much as the average OECD country.[13] Statistics also show that the other wealthy countries generally have better health outcomes with longer life expectancies.[14]

Why is that?

Prices are a significant driver, with costs exceeding general inflation numbers for several reasons. These include the complexity of the U.S. healthcare system, which leads to administrative waste in the insurance and provider payment systems, and the consolidation of hospitals, which can reduce competition or even monopolies, allowing providers to increase prices.

I could continue to cite research for many more pages, but it all boils down to two key conclusions: for healthcare, we are spending more and getting less.

All high-income OECD countries except the U.S. guarantee government or public health coverage for a defined package of covered benefits to all their residents. In addition to public coverage, citizens in several countries have the option to also purchase private coverage. In France, nearly the entire population has both private and public insurance. In contrast, in 2021, 8.6% of the U.S. population was uninsured.[15] The U.S. is the only high-income OECD country where a substantial portion of the population lacks any form of health

---

[13] The Commonwealth Fund. (2023, January 31). *U.S. healthcare from a global perspective, 2022: Accelerating spending, worsening outcomes.* Retrieved August 29, 2025, from https://www.commonwealthfund.org/publications/issue-briefs/2023/jan/us-health-care-global-perspective-2022

[14] Financial Times. (2024, June 11). *America: a healthy or healthcare economy? Financial Times.* Retrieved from https://www.ft.com/content/4a2cfd3b-f692-49df-9857-771e2e39d85b

[15] Organization for Economic Co-operation and Development (OECD). (n.d.). Private health insurance in France. Retrieved August 29, 2025, from https://www.oecd.org/en/publications/private-health-insurance-in-france_555485381821.html

insurance. Despite high U.S. government and private spending, Americans experience worse health outcomes than their peers around the world. For example, life expectancy at birth in the U.S. was 77 years in 2020 — three years lower than the OECD average. Provisional data shows life expectancy in the U.S. dropped even further in 2021.

In America, average life expectancy masks jarring racial and ethnic disparities. Average life expectancy in 2019 for non-Hispanic Black Americans (74.8 years) and non-Hispanic American Indians or Alaska Natives (71.8 years) is four and seven years lower, respectively, than it is for non-Hispanic whites (78.8 years).[16] These realities expose a broken system where social determinants and economic motives collide, hurting the most vulnerable first.

Social factors like poverty and limited access to care worsen outcomes, while a for-profit insurance system prioritizes profits over prevention. [17]This places tremendous stress, not only on our medical system, but also on those who rely on it.

Affordability remains the top reason why some Americans forgo health coverage, while high out-of-pocket costs lead nearly half of working-age adults to skip or delay getting needed care. In the U.S., high prices for health services continue to be the primary driver of this elevated spending. I want to quote this paragraph in their report: "The findings of our international comparison demonstrate the importance of a healthcare system that supports chronic disease prevention and

---

[16] Centers for Disease Control and Prevention, National Center for Health Statistics. (2023). *National vital statistics report: United States life tables, 2021* (NCHS Report No. 72-12). U.S. Department of Health and Human Services. Retrieved from https://www.cdc.gov/nchs/data/nvsr/nvsr72/nvsr72-12.pdf

[17] The Commonwealth Fund. (2023, January 31). *U.S. healthcare from a global perspective, 2022:Accelerating spending, worsening outcomes* [Issue Brief]. Retrieved August 29, 2025, from https://www.commonwealthfund.org/publications/issue-briefs/2023/jan/us-health-care-global-perspective-2022

management, the early diagnosis and treatment of medical problems, affordable access to healthcare coverage, and cost containment — among the key functions of a high-performing system. Other countries have found ways to do these things well; the U.S. can as well."[18]

The last sentence particularly resonates with me. U.S. policymakers and health systems could look to some of the approaches taken by other nations to contain overall health spending, including healthcare and administrative costs. A powerful policy solution to address these dire health outcomes is to implement comprehensive community investment programs that tackle social determinants of health directly. This involves improving housing, access to nutritious food, safe neighborhoods, and quality education, areas proven to reduce health disparities by creating conditions where healthy choices become easier and more accessible for all.

We keep hearing, particularly from our government representatives, that we can't change our system. I'd like to ask why not? The reason we hear that changing the healthcare system is impossible largely boils down to the tremendous influence of insurance companies over lawmakers and policy decisions.

Third Way drew the following conclusion: The 6.7 million working-age Americans facing crushing out-of-pocket costs are caught in a dangerous coverage gap with almost no real protection from year-after-year medical bills. The country needs a universal cost cap that doesn't just limit what people pay in a single bad year, but shields those who are hit with high costs over and over.

---

[18] Commonwealth Fund. (2024, September 19). *Mirror, Mirror 2024: A Portrait of the Failing U.S. Health System* [Report]. Retrieved August 29, 2025, from https://www.commonwealthfund.org/sites/default/files/2024-09/Blumenthal_mirror_mirror_2024_final_v2.pdf

A multi-year cost cap of the kind Third Way proposes would finally put a hard ceiling on what families owe, no matter where they get their insurance or how often they get sick. By tying that cap to income and extending it across multiple years, the policy would strip out the current unfairness where older, sicker, lower-income patients routinely pay a far higher share of their earnings just to stay alive.

Commercial insurance companies wield considerable financial power through lobbying, campaign contributions, and a complex web of regulatory influence, which creates a powerful incentive to maintain the status quo rather than pursue reforms that might reduce their profits. This entrenchment makes meaningful change difficult, as political will succumbs to economic interests rather than prioritizing patients' needs. I'm afraid the only answer might be, "Because we don't want to cut into the insurance companies' profits."[19]

---

[19] The American Medical Association (AMA), Statista, a highly regarded global statistics platform, the Kaiser Family Foundation, the Rand Corporation, Third Way, The Commonwealth Fund, the Peter G. Peterson Foundation, and various government sites, including Medicare.

CHAPTER 9

Epiphany

The for-profit insurance system rewarded volume over value, pushing physicians to do more with less. When taking orthopedic trauma calls, Marc could easily work 100-hour weeks or more. Unfortunately, because of disgraceful reimbursement strategies, our practice might not be paid for every surgery he performs. The erratic reimbursement patterns create a sense of shame and embarrassment for the provider. At the same time, Marc faced resistance from insurers, whose profit-driven priorities often conflicted with providing comprehensive care for orthopedic patients. The healthcare system appeared to be penalizing the doctor for trying to do the work he is trained to do.

In an ideal system, doctors and other healthcare workers should expect and receive timely financial support from the insurers who receive premiums to pay claims. The Hippocratic Oath binds every clinician, but conversely, the insurer is bound by profit margins, its shareholders, and the invisible hands of healthcare.

The night Marc walked into the operating room to treat a patient's fracture, even the nurse anesthetist on-call with him failed to live up to the Hippocratic Oath, personifying the toxic work environment instead.

In the 21st century, healthcare has seen a seismic shift to a for-profit model. As detailed earlier, Adam Smith, the eighteenth-century Scottish economist and moral philosopher, described the free market system as *The Invisible Hand,* using the phrase as a metaphor to describe the unseen forces of self-interest that impact the free market. In theory, consumers basing decisions on self-interest create a positive outcome for the economy. In the practice of medicine, it hasn't worked out that way.

Canada, Great Britain, Germany, and the Scandinavian countries all have different healthcare systems. Canada has multiple providers and the same payor; Germany has several providers and payors, while the U.K. has a single payer and provider. Patients in Shanghai, China, pay a flat percentage of healthcare costs ranging from 10–20%.

And then there's the United States, essentially the wild, wild west of healthcare. We have multiple types of providers: not-for-profit, for-profit, private equity-backed for-profit, private practices, federally qualified health centers; basically, anything goes in terms of the patient care setting, the payor, and the patient outcome. In terms of the payors, it's even wilder due to the lack of regulations. It's the epitome of capitalism.

My "aha moment" in all this came when I realized the American healthcare system is working exactly as it was intended to work. As a doctor, how do you grapple with that, with the realization that this is the way American healthcare is meant to operate?

The shareholders of the insurance companies have priority. They're making money. If patients have private insurance, they're paying their premiums, and at the same time, more financial responsibility is being downloaded on them. Patient copays and deductibles are increasing exponentially, and patients must recognize that healthcare insurance must be part of their personal budget.

Meanwhile, healthcare providers, especially those in private practice, are routinely only being compensated for a fraction of the work they do.

When we have to contact our patients six months after their care to inform them that their insurer still has not paid their bill, they are shocked. They don't know what's going on. Most patients assume their healthcare has been paid for by their insurance.

We clinicians continue to regularly see huge delays in payments, up to 120 days or more, and we may think a payment is in process, but we don't discover until 90 days later that the claim will ultimately be denied. Only after waiting three months are we forced to inform the patient that their insurer has denied their medical claim.

We plead. "Can you call your insurance? There's nothing we've done wrong. We have done everything right. We've gone through the utilization management protocol. We had prior authorization. We have jumped through every hoop, and still, we have not been compensated."

Generally, the insurer gives us a generic reason for rejecting a claim. However, the reason does not have to be accurate. They might say we submitted a duplicate claim, or perhaps we entered an incorrect CPT code, or we didn't follow through on their idiosyncratic requirements on how to code.

In some cases, Marc might be at the trauma center treating a rare injury that would occur perhaps only once or twice a year in our area. A patient may have been in a motorcycle accident with an arm almost severed from the rest of his body. That's a precise, scapular injury that needs immediate, limb-saving surgery. But the code could be denied by insurance because it's uncommon or unusual. Or the insurer might say outright, "We won't pay for that code." But the code is in the book for a reason. It represents a real surgery that may need to be performed in an extreme, but infrequent, circumstance.

At the point of an unjust insurance denial like this one, we must hire an attorney to get insurance reimbursement for the eight-hour-long, but infrequent procedure. Reattaching an arm to a body is a long surgery that requires a high level of expertise because these are injuries to nerves, vessels, bones—all of it. Limb-saving surgery is expensive, and the insurers don't want to pay.

So, they say, "We won't recognize that code."

It's probably closer to the truth to say they, "don't like that code."

The question that begs to be answered is, "Should healthcare be for-profit?"

Fundamentally, I agree it should operate as a non-profit. I'm so deeply involved in the system; I find it hard to envision the practicality of extracting our healthcare from profit-based organizations like commercial insurers. Yet the evidence keeps pointing in one direction: when profit incentives drive care, efficiency, equity, and trust all erode.

A not-for-profit model doesn't eliminate financial responsibility; it redefines success around outcomes, access, and community health instead of margins. Physicians regain autonomy to serve patients rather than shareholders, and resources flow where they improve lives, not quarterly reports. The transition would be complex, but the cost of maintaining the status quo—in burnout, inequity, and lost public trust—is higher still. Healthcare works that way in so many different countries and cultures, but here in the United States, we are entrenched in this predatory, for-profit healthcare system.

Why?

I'll go back to Adam Smith's invisible hand. Healthcare is an industry, or sector, where there is money to be made by private investment. Middle-income people have financial resources that collectively generate profits for major corporations and significant returns to shareholders. And yes, those corporations do provide American workers jobs and are a significant part of the economy. Healthcare is the major employer in almost all of the 50 United States.

But when you look at the largest beneficiaries of federal contracts and grants, the healthcare insurance institutions are in the top 10. Americans are paying taxes, and then on top of that, private insurance premiums, and the government taxes paid are also going to the independent companies that are making extreme profits for their shareholders.

The federal government is complicit in this broken system, and that's the lynchpin.

The United States spends more on healthcare than other top-tier countries. In 2022, the U.S. spent $12,742 per person on healthcare, which was more than double the average for other wealthy countries. And that figure increases every year.

Granted, Americans have access to cutting-edge healthcare. We also fund discoveries, innovations, and opportunities to have, as an example, CyberKnife for prostate cancer care. Those opportunities are more accessible in the U.S. than elsewhere.[1]

However, that doesn't change the fact that the government is complicit. Managed Medicare and Medicaid government plans have become a health domain where insurers can be duplicitous with the government, billing for services that were not provided or overbilling for services that were provided. Taking calculated risks, they would rather pay the fine for violating the law than bill correctly. Meanwhile, the government would also rather continue with managed care plans where companies violate legislation and pay the corporations more than the cost of care, rather than manage the care themselves.

Again, it's time to ask why.

---

[1] Peterson Foundation. (2022, August 19). *How much does the U.S. healthcare system compare to other countries?* Peter G. Peterson Foundation. Retrieved August 29, 2025, from https://www.pgpf.org/article/how-does-the-us-healthcare-system-compare-to-other-countries/

For that answer, you probably need to ask, "What's in it for the legislators who make these decisions?"

According to the Federal Election Commission data, healthcare insurers spent $154,727,479 on lobbying during the 2023-2024 election cycle.[2] I doubt they were lobbying to lower patient premium costs or to reimburse doctors' practices more promptly.

The Supreme Court has also weighed in against patients, increasing the freedom of lobbyists with deep pockets to spend more dollars on policy issues, influencing legislators. As a result, it is standard practice for private insurers to influence healthcare legislation and how healthcare dollars are spent in America. There is no other explanation for legislators' interest in expanding managed Medicare and Medicaid plans, considering documented fraud, overcharges, and abuse.

Patients with managed Medicare and Medicaid plans have another challenge. While some patients may be able to see their primary care provider, despite shortages in family and internal medicine, finding in-network specialists or therapists remains a complex problem. We may see patients who are part of a managed plan, but when we want to refer them to therapy, we often can't get the approval.

Esther, an older patient, came to our practice with severe knee arthritis. For her to be approved by her insurance for a total knee replacement she desperately needed, she would first have to have prior authorization. To obtain that, she would need conservative treatment first, including physical therapy. But because Esther has a managed Medicare plan, she'll have trouble finding a physical therapist who participates with her insurance plan, and she can't get the total knee replaced until she completes a course of therapy.

---

[2] InvestmentInformant. (2024, March 12). Insurance industry ranks 3rd in lobbying spending in 2023. *Repairer Driven News*. Retrieved from https://www.repairerdrivennews.com/2024/03/12/statista-insurance-industry-ranks-3rd-in-lobbying-spending-in-2023/

We are told that this policy exists because this process, by requiring Esther to undergo conservative treatments, such as physical therapy, before the surgery can be authorized, slows things down. "This step ensures that less invasive options are explored prior to moving forward with surgery, aligning care with insurance guidelines and optimizing outcomes." But if she cannot find a therapist who is on panel with her insurance plan with disgraceful reimbursement practices, Esther will never have knee replacement surgery.

Classic Catch-22.

We can't fault the physical therapist. Why would therapists want to be affiliated with a commercial insurer that doesn't pay in a timely manner, or at all? That's not a long-term strategy for physical therapy practice success.

If, by chance, we can get Esther physical therapy, we can check the box for conservative treatment.

Until then, she is ineligible for a total joint replacement. Even though Esther is a senior citizen with bone-on-bone arthritis, severe deformity, and limited ability to walk independently, those radiographic and clinical criteria mean nothing without an attempted course of less invasive treatment.

As surgeons, having gone through the United States medical training system, we are conditioned to cope with the limitations of the system we have been given.

In cases where our patient has multiple medical issues, we will prioritize and address all necessary treatments to ensure comprehensive care. Our mission is to help the patient. That is my focus: not how I feel about it, but what I can do for the patient in front of me.

I can't afford to be outraged by the system, or I'd be throwing 10 "hissy fits" a day. I must put all my energy into helping patients like Esther get her total knee replacement surgery.

This is one of the reasons the system perpetuates itself. As a doctor, I wasn't trained to fight the system or tell the United States' legislators and administrators to course correct and reexamine how healthcare dollars are being spent.

Bucking America's healthcare system is not in my wheelhouse.

My orthopedic wheelhouse is this: Esther has a deformity in her knee alignment. She has a limited range of motion in her knee joint and a limited ability to ambulate without an assistive device, a cane, or a walker. Esther needs a total knee replacement. However, to get paid, I've been told that she must try a conservative treatment that I know is not going to work. Dollars must be spent there first. Then I can do the surgery I have been trained to do.

I have not been trained to examine the system, and I'm not trained to have feelings about it. That effort, several times each day, would result in psychological overload.

To a certain extent, the American public is bamboozled by medical shows on television where everyone rushes to help the sick and wounded, with never a question about insurance or affordability. Doctors and surgeons have countless hours to spend with a patient, with emotions on full display on television, not in real life.

In fact, doctors who do not handle their own practice billing are often unaware of what is really happening with medical finances. They outsource their billings and collections and never fully understand the details, causing delays.

Those physicians working for hospitals know about the care they provide, and they may know about the bully that doesn't want them to handle the case at 2 a.m., but they're not aware of the invisible, money-grubbing bullies acting behind the scenes. They don't know about the other pieces of the puzzle that lead up to delayed compensation.

Because I want to know how things work and because I'm detail-oriented and stubborn, I chose to uncover information that far too many health professionals are unaware of when it comes to how healthcare dollars are spent.

And because I now know what's going on, I feel compelled to share that knowledge.

This is important.

Had I chosen to work in a hospital or a large academic practice, I might never have unearthed everything I now know. Before I joined my husband, he didn't know because he was completely focused on the surgery side of medicine and left the finances to his business office.

I had the luxury of being aligned with Marc. While he was rowing the boat and keeping the practice afloat, I had time to delve into how the financial side of the practice worked. I also happen to have an affinity for business. I have a mind that can understand and assess what's in front of me without getting distracted by red herrings.

One way to look at the problem with the healthcare system as it exists in America today is that we are treating healthcare as a profitable commodity. And that goes right back to Adam Smith's invisible hand.

In theory, the system could work if we had regulations that protected the patient from practices that are not beneficial to their health. But we are so far along the pathway of prior authorization and utilization management that we can't help but see some form of harm to the patient, antithetical to the Hippocratic Oath.

Earlier, I identified the insurance companies as the enemy, but in truth, it goes beyond that. The antagonist is the for-profit, capitalist nature of the system. When profit margins depend on the misfortune of others, healthcare surely must be identified as a breed of disaster capitalism.

But this is not just sick care we're talking about. We also need wellness care, with annual exams and screenings. But by charging high out-of-pocket fees and enforcing waiting periods, insurers are working directly against the well-being of the patient. Prior authorizations force patients to wait, and sometimes they're waiting for care that is necessary to prevent the worsening of the disease, especially when it comes to cancer. If insurers are enforcing a waiting period for someone who has a fast-growing tumor that can kill them, they are, by definition, gambling with a patient's life.

That is parasitic.

The healers who are providing the care also must wait for compensation for work they have already done, and that's a fundamental issue for our practice. Healthcare providers are closing because they can't operate under those constraints. They need a steady flow of income, or they will shut their doors.

When insurers layer the waiting periods on top of the other strategies they employ to maximize return to their shareholders, we have a system with only one purpose: profit through suffering.

Healthcare has been commodified.

Stories circulate about people who go bankrupt paying their healthcare costs.[3] An example story illustrating how people go bankrupt paying healthcare costs is that of Sherrie and Michael Foy from Virginia. After Michael retired, Sherrie had colon surgery with complications leading to nearly $800,000 in medical bills from the University of Virginia Health System, which their insurance did not cover. Unable to pay, the Foys declared bankruptcy, having depleted their savings, cashed in a life insurance policy, and even liquidated accounts meant for their grandchildren. The bankruptcy drastically altered their lives, as they

---

[3] Levey, N., Pattani, A., Noguchi, Y., & Sable-Smith, B. (2022, December 21). *Medical debt upended their lives. here's what it took from them.* NPR. https://www.npr.org/sections/health-shots/2022/06/16/1104969627/medical-debt-upended-their-lives-heres-what-it-took-from-them

now get by on Michael's pension and Social Security, while facing ongoing health challenges in the family.[4]

When an insurer denies a claim, the bill still must be paid.

In our practice, we don't pass the entire bill along to the patient, but larger facilities will, hoping the patient can and will pay. The hospital might also choose not to fight or appeal against the denial and go to the patient instead because it is easier than hiring attorneys to fight insurance companies for them. In some cases, the patient is underinsured and is simultaneously responsible for a large copay or deductible.

As far as the patient is concerned, the game is rigged.

---

[4] Satija, N. (2022, June 16). *100 million people in America are saddled with medical debt*. The Texas Tribune.
https://www.texastribune.org/2022/06/16/americans-medical-debt/

CHAPTER 10

Crisis

In 2014, I was 43. I'd battled two severe viral lung infections that spring and summer, but I fully recovered and was feeling generally well. It was summertime. Our children were eight and 10. My routine that summer was to wake up by 3:30 or 4 a.m. to meditate and pray, do my workout at the local gym at 5 a.m., and then come home in time to get the kids up, have breakfast together, and drive them to their 7:45 a.m. bus for summer day camp.

On this particular morning, I woke up as usual, swung my legs over the bed, stood, and almost collapsed, overwhelmed with a feeling of fatigue. With legs like Jell-O, I tried to walk through the master closet to our bathroom. However, even this simple task felt insurmountable. I couldn't move. I reached my hands back to the mattress, steadied myself, and plopped back down.

My life changed that day.

I tried to decipher what was happening. Was I just tired? Was I dehydrated? I wasn't in pain, but I had no energy. Something serious was going on. I mentally scanned my body from head to toe for signs of illness or localized discomfort and found nothing.

I attempted to get up, to stand again. And then again. And then a fourth time. At this point, I was more puzzled than afraid, although a small grain of fear began to form, lurking somewhere in the back of my mind.

There had to be an explanation.

My medical training kicked in. I analyzed the functional aspects of what was occurring. What was it going to take for me to get up?

I woke Marc up. "I don't know exactly what's going on," I said. "I feel a little tired."

He went to our closet and pulled out my old doctor's bag containing the blood pressure cuff I'd used all four years of med school. But surprisingly, he had a tough time getting a read. I had to have a blood pressure, right? Well, we hadn't used the sphygmomanometer in years, so it wasn't a surprise that it no longer worked.

Finally, with Marc's help, I was able to get out of bed, walk to the bathroom, and get myself dressed. I dragged myself down the stairs to the kitchen, holding onto the banister and taking cautious, awkward steps. Once downstairs, I dropped onto the couch in our formal living room.

There was no way I would be able to perform the surgery scheduled for that morning. Marc agreed to go to the surgery center in my place and explain to the patients that he would be their surgeon that day.

When the kids finally came bouncing down the stairs, I lifted my head from the cushion and told them to make themselves some cereal and pour some orange juice. It was a fine summer day, and the kids needed to get to Deerkill Day Camp, so I cautiously drove them to the bus's pickup location in Hoboken, the next town. I leaned the seat way back, so I was almost lying down, instructed them to walk to the bus, being careful to stay on the sidewalk, and then I waved them off as I watched them climb on board.

I absolutely could not walk them to the bus, and I still have no idea how I managed to even drive there, let alone drive myself back home.

While I was in the car, Marc called to let me know our cardiologist, whose office was five minutes from our house, was available to see me. Later that morning, again with great caution, I drove to the cardiologist's office, parked, got out of the car, and staggered in a wavy zigzagging line to the door.

The worried look I got from an elderly lady passing by with her shopping cart told me she probably thought I was drunk.

Once inside the office, the medical assistants immediately hooked me up to the EKG machine, taking my blood pressure at the same time. My blood pressure and my heart rate were far too low. The cardiologist's diagnosis was instant, "You have a junctional rhythm," he said. "Erica, I need you to go to the hospital. I am admitting you to the Cardiac Critical Care Unit (CCU)."

A junctional rhythm is an irregular heartbeat that occurs when the heart's natural pacemaker isn't working properly.

"I'm not going to the hospital right now," I insisted. "I have to go home and pack a bag. And, no, I'm not going in an ambulance either."

Marc made his way home after handling my surgery that morning and arrived about the same time I did. After I packed a few items, he gently ushered me into his car and drove me to the hospital, where they admitted me directly to the CCU.

Once at the hospital, my analytical mind started working on all cylinders. I was dizzy, weak, and just generally not feeling well. But I had more information now: seriously low blood pressure and low heart rate. Was this life-threatening? Maybe. Once the CCU staff stabilized my condition, completed their initial examination, and the cardiac-specific group of blood tests, I wondered what more I would be subjected to?

I sent my friend, Sonja, a surgical tech, a quick text. "I'm in the CCU."

She texted back, "Why are you in the CCU? That's not your floor!"

"I've been admitted. I'm a patient."

As soon as her shift was over, Sonja rushed to my room. She was a genius at making people laugh, and I was no exception. Even in my current state, I giggled at her silly jokes and her gossipy stories of everything that was going on in the OR suite. The comic relief only she could offer was just what I needed.

Later that day, I woke up from a light doze to see a large man entering my room. He introduced himself as the hospital chaplain and asked if he could pray for me. I spoke a little Spanish, but, for some reason, I had a bit of difficulty grasping the chaplain's specific Spanish accent and had to concentrate fully to understand him.

"Why are you here?" he asked.

I told him, "I have a busy career as a surgeon, two children, no local extended family support, and I think I may have over-extended myself."

"Then this is your opportunity to reflect," he said. "Now, here, in this room, you will look in the mirror and decide if you like what you see. And then maybe you will tell yourself why you are really here."

And then we prayed, while his words echoed in my head.

I was hooked up to a cardiac monitor that beeped constantly because my heart rate was 23, far below even an athlete's resting rate of over 40. A normal heart rate is 60–100. The nurses finally had to silence the alarms because the beeping was constant.

The CCU nurses continued to measure my blood pressure and heart rate while giving me intravenous fluids and electrolytes. Slowly, my heart rate crept into the fourties. Two days later, after doing a trans esophageal echocardiogram and a cardiac stress test to confirm my heart was structurally fine, I was discharged, and Marc brought me home.

Fortunately, my heart had no structural defects; however, an underlying electrical conduction abnormality, undetectable by previous EKGs, had lain dormant until then.

After this episode, my cardiac condition didn't allow me to stand for hours in an operating room, and I learned I would need to give up what I had trained for and felt called to do. It had taken me a heroic amount of work to become a surgeon. Leaving that behind was tough on so many levels.

We all know stress can exacerbate any heart condition, and I'm convinced the stress and demands of dealing with the adversarial insurance companies every day were contributing factors to my condition. I suspect I also had a genetic predisposition for it, but the amount of stress I faced certainly had a serious impact, and because of my heart's inability to withstand stress, I switched roles to become the physician-support/administrator of our practice.

Through all this, I fortunately never had issues with my personal insurance company. Marc and I pay a hefty premium for our top-of-the-line healthcare coverage. I imagine my situation would have been different had I been depending on Medicaid, or even if our insurance had been less than top-tier.

How much you earn and how much you can afford to pay in premiums absolutely affect healthcare outcomes.

Fourteen months after my crisis, to alleviate constant fatigue, I opted to receive a pacemaker to bring my heart rate up to a more normal level, and my daily function to a more normal pace.

My biggest challenge during this crisis was finding a new way to achieve the satisfaction and fulfillment I'd enjoyed when helping patients as a surgeon. In the meantime, I fully embraced being the main caregiver for my children and the financial advisor of the practice.

CHAPTER 11

Mourn and Mend

After I came home from the hospital, I devoted my immediate attention and energy to our family and to getting healthy. I also devoted considerable energy to finding my new normal. How much of my work as a surgeon was I capable of performing? How much exercise could I handle? What was the right diet for me?

It took several months to reach a state of equilibrium, and I slowly began to settle into a new routine. Then, one day, I heard a voice urging me. In my mind, I heard three letters: DTS, DTS, DTS...

Not surprisingly, having been raised in the Christian faith, I wondered if the voice was the Holy Spirit talking to me. But what did DTS mean?

I Googled "DTS" and found *Dallas Theological Seminary, "Where Truth and Love Lead the Way."* I read their website, my heart saying, "Yes!" But while they offered online degree programs, they did not have a fully virtual program in the degree I was interested in studying.

I checked their website periodically, while "DTS" kept echoing in my mind. More than eighteen months later, the course I was looking for came fully online: a Master's in Biblical and Theological Studies. I began the enrollment process, and suddenly I was back on the academic train, asking for official transcripts from college and med school, requesting letters of recommendation from pastors, applying, interviewing, and being accepted.

I dove into my seminary studies, taking multiple classes each semester and writing papers, but at my own pace. Since my childhood, as an elementary school student at Chula Vista Christian School in San Diego, I have been passionate about Bible studies. With this seminary education, I cultivated credibility, confidence, and a solid biblical foundation. I began my new journey in the fall of 2016 and graduated in 2019 as a Master of Biblical and Theological Studies (MBTS). With the dramatic shift my life had taken, the seminary studies gave me purpose and grounded my faith. My time at DTS instilled in me a deep understanding of the historical context of the Bible as well as a strong framework for how to study.

DTS was the perfect seminary, encouraging a fearless approach to supplementary resources to the Bible, including commentaries, digital study tools, and academic source materials. The seminary also exposed me to techniques to utilize emerging technologies and additional references that I didn't already have in my extensive library.

At the end of my seminary program, with my degree confirmed, I gave myself a special gift. I traveled to Oxford University in England to attend a four-week program at the Oxford Centre for Christian Apologetics (OCCA). I discovered OCCA while reading an apologetics book I purchased on Amazon. I applied online, interviewed virtually, and was offered one of 12 places in the business program. While in Oxford, I met an alumnus of my apologetics course who was studying in the Said Business School's Executive MBA program, another item on my bucket list. I'd long wanted to study for an MBA, to understand the business side of healthcare more thoroughly. After capturing my interest, the OCCA alum kindly introduced me to one of the admissions administrators of the Oxford Executive MBA program, who, upon learning of my background, encouraged me to apply. Three months later, I was delighted to receive a letter of admission to the January 2020 cohort.

Oxford was a powerful experience. From a Christian perspective, the history is deep. The Martyr's Square is a monument to those who sacrificed their lives 500 years ago for the Christian faith. So many different versions of the Bible have touched that historic institution. And then, having the opportunity to shift to the business side felt like a spiritual power was guiding my way.

I was able to take a huge step back because I was no longer busy with surgeries. The health crisis that sidelined my career afforded me the time and the distance to analyze what was happening in the practice and to apply what I learned in the MBA to the economics of healthcare. Adding my personal experience to the mix, I acquired the tools and information to make a sound assessment of the current state of healthcare affairs from a private practice perspective.

Returning to the orthopedic practice, my foundations, spiritually and professionally, were stronger than ever. I'd started growing my spiritual foundation from the age of two. My Christian faith was a solid grounding for my choice to become a physician and for practicing medicine the way I did. My faith gave me the values that shaped how I live my life and how I relate to our patients. The MBA also made a tangible difference, expanding my perspective on the business side of medicine and leading to my epiphany, where I truly grasped the adversarial nature of the healthcare system.

I was studying for my MBA when the COVID-19 pandemic came on the scene. Although there was a slight delay in the MBA program, I continued to study virtually until I was able to resume flying to England for a week of in-person instruction.

During my time at Oxford, I developed a tech platform as an entrepreneurial venture, designed to improve operating room supply chain efficiency and sustainability for the implants and instruments we use in orthopedic surgery. At the same time, I was asking, "How can I take what I've learned about healthcare practice, healthcare insurance, and health economics to create something meaningful and influential to advance the broader public conversation?"

This book was the logical next step. But the light bulb didn't go off immediately. It was on a dimmer switch, and it took a while to understand that this was a project I was called to complete.

At the end of 2021, I flew back to England for our MBA commencement, where I was selected by my classmates to be one of three class speakers at the event. Since my time at Oxford, I have seen a continuous erosion of America's healthcare system. Insurance companies have increased their control of the purse in all aspects, including delaying and denying claims without cause to avoid reimbursing facilities and private practices for their work. Commercial insurers continue to build barriers to claims transparency. What should be readily quantifiable has become unimaginable and uninterpretable.

As we've analyzed, the insurer also controls the patient like a marionette, through many laborious requirements, and that goes right back to minimizing costs through utilization management. This is especially frustrating when a patient has a clinically diagnosed disease and cannot receive the care they need and deserve in a timely fashion due to strict prior authorization policies and gatekeeping.

It continues to get worse. We see prior authorization and utilization management strategies expanding beyond diagnostic studies to include surgery, oncology, and other life-saving treatments, even encompassing pharmaceuticals.

We're even noticing prior authorization requirements creeping into dictating where patients can receive their care. In decades past, patients were discouraged from receiving surgeries in ambulatory care facilities. Now, in an about-face, insurance companies demand that patients receive their care in those centers because they generally cost less. In peer-to-peer conversations, where we attempt to reverse denials of care for our patients, we have been told that surgeries will not be authorized if they are performed in certain hospital facilities but will be authorized if the location of surgery is changed to a stand-alone surgery center. One patient had two carpal tunnel surgeries. Our practice was told that the second surgery had to be performed in a different, stand-alone surgical facility if authorization was to be obtained. It's nonsensical.

Prior authorization requirements ensure patients can't receive care at the time of diagnosis, to delay care, waiting periods are being strictly enforced, and certain facilities are being excluded.

As I mentioned, orthopedic surgeons are told that specific criteria must be met before patients can obtain imaging studies, physical therapy, or definitive surgical care. For example, requirements for physical therapy before they can have an MRI, and prior authorizations on top of prior authorizations. One such patient did not have the out-of-network benefits that would allow us to do his surgery, but because he needed the care, we requested and received a single-case agreement type prior authorization, which allowed him to stay with our practice. However, after the surgery was performed, our practice was informed that because the patient did not have the out-of-network benefit, we would not be reimbursed for the surgery, for which we obtained a single-case prior authorization. In this way, the insurer successfully shifted the cost of surgery to the patient.

Once again, we observed that prior authorization does not guarantee payment.

Only when patients have exhaustive insurance coverage information can they properly budget for healthcare.

And it's a patient's *right* to know.

Insurers should share policy information freely, including detailed summaries of plan benefits. If patients don't know their summary healthcare benefits, they don't know the accompanying financial responsibility. Becoming seriously ill could result in insurmountable debt.

When providers request plan documentation pertaining to the cost of care for our patients, we invariably will not receive the entire summary of plan benefits. Even if we're clear with the insurer that we are requesting plan information on behalf of our patient, the insurer requires that our patient make the request. Sometimes, insurance companies even insist that patients cannot make their request in writing! Patients must make a telephone call, and yes, they will be placed on hold. Even after requesting by phone, commercial insurance subscribers may wait weeks for the vital information.

So, where do we go from here? We cannot continue the present trajectory without dire consequences for both healthcare providers and their patients.

We can inform the public about the situation, which will lead to dialogue and conversation, which should lead to solutions. Or will it? The fact is, the public can be well informed, as they are about a raft of crises affecting our lives today, and, as we've seen, being informed doesn't necessarily mean that a dialogue will take place, and it certainly doesn't guarantee action or policy change.

People are overwhelmed: climate change, mass shootings, hurricanes, wildfires, and political upheaval. Understandably, they feel helpless. What can one individual do? The easiest answer tends to be, grab a beverage and pick up the remote.

Still, healthcare providers' first step must be informing the public.

That's the purpose of this book. But when policy changes are necessary, we have to create the mechanisms to effect that. We already have one: the American Medical Association (AMA), a broadly subscribed and well-funded group. But where is their voice? I hear crickets.

National organizations like the AMA should be on the front lines of the healthcare battle, yet here I am, in a boutique private practice, feeling like I'm a lone, cogent voice in the wilderness.

Through online searches, I found articles in peer-reviewed journals quantifying the myriad problems with prior authorization in medical care, but I don't see tangible action being taken. I was recently asked by a CBS news correspondent to comment on a patient's letter to the news station. The patient was asking for help as she could not obtain the medication prescribed by her hematologist. Her physician's requests for prior authorization had been denied three times.

Apparently, this patient thought the media was more effective than public servants. If our legislators have the information, the peer-reviewed data, they have a civic obligation to do something. We need to change the healthcare system to benefit the patient.

The word "socialism" has become a dog whistle that instills fear in the public, and the phrase "socialized medicine" does the same. But I'm not making a case for socialized anything. I'm advocating for regulations of the system. We have to stop predatory practices. We must redirect our healthcare model toward transparent systems that value patient outcomes over profit margins. Breaking up monopoly control in the medical supply chain is essential to restoring fairness, affordability, and integrity in care.

It feels as if no one in "power" wants to change, but the reality is that, because of soaring costs, the face of healthcare is changing whether we want it to or not. Rural and urban hospitals and healthcare facilities are bankrupt. Many are closing and leaving patients without access. Thousands of rural patients no longer have local to tertiary care staples like interventional cardiology or emergent stroke care.

Whether we choose to legislate change or not, the system is getting more unaffordable.

The question is, who do we want in charge? The insurance companies or the medical professionals? Do patients want their voices heard?

Will we shape the future of health through action or be swept aside?

CHAPTER 12

Ethos, Pathos, Logos, and Strategies to Safely Cope

If we want to cope with the invisible hand in healthcare, we must first accept that there are significant emotions attached to the strings of the invisible hand. As either patient or physician, our psychological safety is tenuous. Because we encounter uncertainty in so many dimensions of the finance of medicine, we are emotionally vulnerable. As physicians, we are trained to expect variables related to our patients' disease process, the limitations of medications, surgeries, and our present knowledge. But, doing this work under the specter of added financial pressure with the literal shadow of the invisible hand instilling unease, anxiety, and overwhelm is a superhuman task.

I know.

Before my pacemaker surgery, I was taking care of my patients and simultaneously managing our practice finances. I would often wonder why it was taking increasingly longer to receive reimbursements for care from insurance companies. To pay our practice expenses, Marc and I, at times, could not pay ourselves. We used our savings to fill in the gaps. And after speaking with other doctors, I discovered we were not alone.

For the money to pay for the cost of healthcare to get to the providers of care, be it healthcare systems, macro, or small practices like ours, micro, the premiums patients pay must be filtered through insurance companies.

That's the ethos, the milieu, the environment of the current crisis in healthcare.

Before my cardiac episode, I felt vulnerable financially because I had yet to create a vocabulary for the threat of the third-party insurer's playbook: deny and delay. Each day, my thoughts turned inward. "What am I doing wrong?" My sanity was strangled by the invisible hand as it restricted the flow of funds to our practice. We were still working hard, still seeing full office hours. As in any company, those of us who practice medicine view our revenues as oxygen. Finding my practice firmly within the grip of insurers, as they denied or delayed payments, stifled me.

The invisible hand in medicine, whether we like it or not, is a credible, consistent threat. Recognizing on the front end that every third-party payer has their fingers on the oxygen valve, that they have the power to strangle your practice, and by extension your mentality, is a game-changer. It is a nimble threat to our livelihoods, the medical practice environment, and our sanity. Therefore, it must be handled as we would deal with any other dangerous liaison: with preparation, documentation, and agile strategy.

The realization that my cardiac condition was in no small part due to the suffocation of my practice by erratic reimbursement and payment structures led me to examine the construct I believed to exist in American medicine and to measure it against reality. When I started my medical career, I believed medicine was egalitarian. A sector where we do "good work" for all our patients with thoughtful care. If we are lucky, our patients may even find full recovery or a cure. Through readily accessible diagnostics, medical and surgical interventions, we safely deliver our patients, those under our care, to wellness. As a Hopkins medical student, I was granted permission to focus on the patient, the task of healing, and my patient's medical journey.

"We hold these truths to be self-evident that all men are created equal with certain unalienable rights..." At the beginning of my career, I thought I was on the side of life, liberty, and the pursuit of happiness, offering credible consultations in my patients' best interests. I saw myself as a valued stakeholder supporting a patient's unalienable right to life, a professional, highly trained, and highly educated. But tell me, who can do this work without being compensated in proportion to their financial, emotional, and educational investment?

Through the protections of the current system, the insurers say, "Don't worry about the financial aspects. Do everything you can, altruistically, at great personal sacrifice, and we will pay on the back end." Nothing could be further from the truth.

In conversation with an ER attending recently, we lamented the demands and sacrifices doctors made during the COVID-19 pandemic. Emergency attendings were asked to work double shifts, without proper personal protective equipment, and then, when the institutions received compensation, federal bonuses, no additional financial compensation to doctors and caregivers was forthcoming. Instead, the emergency room attendings and their family members were asked to pay several hundred dollars for COVID tests administered at work.

I've detailed the hurdles to being paid on the "back end."

The invisible hand is an illusionist, a magician, leading doctors through a minefield of false constructs. I've detailed the fallacies in a previous chapter. As we follow these falsehoods through the established path, we find ourselves in the land of medical make-believe, rife with wrong narratives. Medical providers, like myself, are highly trained, skilled professionals. How long am I supposed to wait for compensation for the work I have done? One year, two? Our practice has hired attorneys to mediate our cases, and subsequently, we have received favorable decisions. And yet, frequently we wait as long as two to three years for insurers to comply with a judge's decision in our favor and directive to pay within 30 days.

In the first half of 2025, we physicians were dealt a major blow by the Texas Fifth Circuit Court of Appeals. The decision supported 'deny and delay', lack of payment, or delayed payment by third-party insurers. The court essentially ruled that physicians do not have the right to sue carriers for overdue payments.

Decisions like these remind me to stop looking in the wrong direction. I could easily interpret such a decision as devaluing my life's work as a doctor.

I cannot afford to be naively optimistic, and similarly, I must be honest about the invisible hand's illusion that if I do everything I can for a patient, I will be compensated. Instead, I must use data to clarify and cultivate an accurate image of the invisible hand and its associated stakeholders. I find myself constantly seeking to protect my practice and myself in an environment rife with threats. For my patients, I am often the victim of overfamiliarity and a sense of entitlement, a thought that my doctor is at fault, not my insurance company. Every day, we encounter at least one patient in our practice who undervalues our work. The PR campaigns that Wendell Potter alluded to are working.

Pathologically, patients suffer. While insurance companies like Cigna, UnitedHealthcare, and Humana are facing legal consequences for processing claims with AI algorithms and denying care in batches, patients are often burdened with unnecessary costs or denied necessary care.[1]

This is the pathos, the problem in healthcare.

I want patients to understand the motivators in healthcare. This book is painting a picture of the healthcare environment, so everyone, patients and doctors, can look at this problem and not ignore it until we need it, and then experience immense frustration because we find our healthcare system really isn't what we thought it was. Why wait until we get the big "C", cancer diagnosis, or until we have an elderly family member with a hip fracture that needs to be fixed? We want to try to get on the front end of this, right?

To survive in medicine, one must expect and be prepared for extensive gate-keeping measures, prior authorization requirements, and limited patient access to in-network resources. To survive, one must walk into healthcare, understanding that on the 'back end,' our work or our health will be financially undervalued.

As doctors, documenting each patient encounter allows us to accurately assess the complex medical landscape. We scour the latest resistance strategies implemented against providers. We anticipate system failures. We engage more candidly with our patients regarding the financial aspects of their care, even with insurance.

We doctors are often told when a prior authorization is denied, "We are not denying care. We are not authorizing payment for care." Our responsibility is then to engage the patient in the conversation. Often, as physicians, we feel that hitting this brick wall is an individual critique. We feel this pressure is too heavy and in direct conflict with the goal of preventing adverse patient outcomes.

---

[1] David S. Greenberg, D. A. R. (2023, December 22). *Health insurers sued over use of artificial intelligence to deny medical claims*. ArentFox Schiff. https://www.afslaw.com/perspectives/health-care-counsel-blog/health-insurers-sued-over-use-artificial-intelligence-deny

We believe that while advocating for others, we must also advocate for ourselves. We validate our practice's worth by continuing to hold ourselves to the highest standard.

We also accept that every stakeholder (business speak for player) in medicine is looking out for his or her self-interest first. The invisible hand is not accountable to the patient in the same way our practice is accountable for adverse outcomes. We are responsible for our decisions. We are not responsible for the insurance company's decision not to pay for healthcare. We are not responsible for the insurer's decision to override our treatment plan. We will continue to reaffirm and know that integrity, character, and concerns for patient outcomes are what make our practice great.

Our practice, unlike many insurance companies, is not focused solely on where money can be made. We will not allow insurers to use purse strings to create crises without holding the accompanying accountability for patient outcomes. Allowing insurers "zero accountability" is no longer a part of our vocabulary.

If our patients have injuries that require physical therapy, they should know how many sessions they are entitled to and will be covered under their insurance plan. I'll tell you we tried to facilitate this process of creating transparency for our patients in our practice, especially those preparing for total joint replacement surgery. Patients also need to know what costs they will be responsible for, what balance will be attributed to them. In the context of getting aftercare after surgery, is there a co-pay? A deductible? How much cash do patients need to have on hand? We've tried to facilitate, to help our patients obtain this information. Our success rates were not good. We were either told by the insurer that the patient has to request this information on their own, or we were provided with an incomplete document. So, we found that insurers, to whom they paid premiums, gave our patients no response, a partial response, or a delayed response.

We cannot let the currently high levels of opacity, or lack of transparency, and financial intensity, prevent our optimism. We can cultivate hope, create a culture of caring, not just for patients but for ourselves.

I look at this scenario, this ethos and pathos, like a David and Goliath story. There were many days and weeks when David's brothers stood in the Valley of Elah, taunted by the giant Goliath. Even King Saul was taunted by Goliath. And then, one day, David, the meal shuttle, the teenage boy, decides this has to stop. We've had enough. Well, everyone looks at this healthcare crisis with resignation, a "woe is me" attitude. I believe there is one smooth stone that can take down all of the negative, injurious policies and procedures that are strangling the flow of resources from what has the potential to be a phenomenal healthcare system.

I believe we are that David with one smooth stone that will fix this healthcare crisis we are in right now.

We are the logos. We, the people, and our system of laws.

Let's expect the unexpected, adding predictability to the walls we encounter every day. Define for ourselves what is important. We providers must tell the truth. Let patients know, "Your insurer is not saying no. They are just saying they will not pay."

I recommend that, just as we are vigilant about changes in our bodies, we need to be equally observant of our insurer's annual changes in coverage, and we should know what costs are being passed along to us, the subscribers. It is essential that we find the most cost-effective plan for our healthcare needs. I recommend quarterly, semi-annual, and annual check-ins to make sure that our insurance plan benefits have not changed, and that our healthcare providers', or doctors', acceptance of those benefits also remains unchanged. Then, expand that perspective to our extended family, applying the same proactive consumer-based mentality. Make sure we know about the benefits for eldercare, which is often a cause of bankruptcy. Insurance companies have customer service resources to help.

We need to be in the know.

Stop being passive. Look at the share price trends over the last five to 10 years for your insurance company. How much has it increased? That number represents, in some part, the value of your premiums that are being returned to their company's shareholders, their stocks.

Public policy is also important, and it must change for the better. Let's hold our legislators responsible, whether it's at the local, state, or national level. Talk to them about delayed provider reimbursements for healthcare services and unfair utilization management strategies. Inform them of the doctor shortages that are creating 3–4 month wait times for primary care appointments. Let's demand that our government become more proactive in protecting patients from the profit-centered approach of most commercial insurance. Write a letter or send an email. I've included a template in the Appendix: use it, modify it, make it more personal, give a personal example, but do send it.

It may not feel like it right now, but every day people do have the power to change healthcare policy. Insurers are "buying" congressional compliance through lobbying, but patients and voters should also make their voices heard. Why are we consistently paying more for less without congressional oversight? Just understand that we are not the only ones knocking at the legislative door.

We can change our healthcare system to make it work for all of us: patients, doctors, and the healthcare institutions where we receive care.

Let's do it now!

Let's be inclusive, be innovative, be intentional, be prolific, be optimistic.

As Brutus said to Cassius, "Carpe diem."

Seize the day!

Acknowledgments

I am grateful:

To God, the Supreme Author.

To my family, thank you for supporting my endless ambition and serial projects. Dr. Mary F. Rowe, I am grateful for your example of love, resilience, and leadership. Dr. Marc Urquhart, I am grateful for your indulgence, kindness, care, and never-ending commitment. Amari and Alexis, thank you for the joy of seeing a better world through your eyes.

To the collaborators on this book project and the UpMed: *A Journal of Healthcare's Race to the Bottom* podcast, thank you for lending me your ears, for truly listening, and for shaping the story. Goody Lindley, you are a godsend. Jill Ellyn Riley, you have a knack for seeing the potential flaws and steering me away from them. Tim Vandehey, you showed me the importance of utilizing structure and motivation to maximize impact. Nathan Buller, you patiently held my hand when this incredible journey began.

To the author of the insightful article in *The Intelligencer,* who shed light on insurance executive perspectives I would not otherwise have been given access to, your work helped me to provide a more balanced perspective.

To my friends who empathetically listened to my tale of woe. I am so grateful that you never discouraged me, even when I couldn't find the words. In fact, you did the opposite. You shared your stories, your contacts, and your time until I found my voice.

To our patients and staff at Urquhart Orthopedic Associates, thank you for advancing our mission, for seeking care and providing care in an environment of healing, on the cutting-edge, with a personal touch.

You are all the best.

Glossary of Terms

Major insurance terms relevant to this book:

Coinsurance:	Occurs after meeting the deductible when the insured pays a percentage of healthcare expenses known as coinsurance. It is similar to friends in a carpool covering a portion of the gas expense, while the driver also pays a portion. Typically, coinsurance operates on a fixed ratio, meaning the insured will always be charged the same percentage of the total bill each time. Many insurers, like Medicare, operate on an 80/20 coinsurance plan.
Commercial health insurance:	A type of health insurance coverage that companies offer to individuals and businesses. It is different from other types of health insurance, such as Medicare and Medicaid, because it is not sponsored by the government. Commercial health insurance plans offer comprehensive coverage. Also, many commercial health insurance plans offer some preventive care services for free, including screenings, checkups, and immunizations. Commercial health insurance plans can also cover mental health services.
Copay, also called a copayment:	A determined amount of money beneficiaries pay to their healthcare provider for healthcare visits, prescription drugs, and other services. The type of care, such as specialty care or urgent care, determines the copay amount. Generally, copays begin at around $10 and can be as high as $75. Additionally, copays often don't count toward deductibles, meaning individuals pay a copay regardless of whether they've reached their deductible.

CPT (current procedural terminology) codes:	Developed and maintained by the American Medical Association (AMA), are a standardized system used to describe medical, surgical, and diagnostic services, facilitating communication and billing between healthcare providers and payers. CPT codes cover a wide range of medical services, including medical, surgical, radiology, laboratory, anesthesia, genomic sequencing, and evaluation and management (E/M) services. CPT codes are essential for healthcare providers to receive payment or reimbursement for services rendered to patients.
Deductible:	The amount of money that the insured person pays before their insurance policy starts paying for covered expenses.
Government-backed insurance:	Public programs provide the primary source of coverage for most seniors and low-income children and families who meet certain eligibility requirements. The primary public programs are Medicare, a federal social insurance program for seniors (generally persons aged 65 and over) and certain disabled individuals; Medicaid, funded jointly by the federal government and states but administered at the state level, which covers certain low-income children and their families; and CHIP, also a federal-state partnership that serves certain children and families who do not qualify for Medicaid but who cannot afford private coverage. Other public programs include military health benefits provided through TRICARE and the Veterans Health Administration, and benefits provided through the Indian Health Service. Some states have additional programs for low-income individuals. In 2011, approximately 60% of stays were billed to Medicare and Medicaid, up from 52% in 1997.

ICD (diagnosis) codes:	Specifically ICD-10-CM is a standardized system used by healthcare providers to code diseases and medical conditions for diagnosis and billing purposes. ICD stands for International Classification of Diseases, and the "10" refers to the 10th revision of the classification system. The "CM" stands for Clinical Modification, indicating that these codes are used in a clinical setting in the United States.
	Purpose: These codes are used to classify and code diseases, injuries, and other health problems for various purposes, including
	• Diagnosis: Healthcare providers use ICD codes to document a patient's diagnosis.
	• Billing: ICD codes are used for billing purposes, helping to determine what services are covered and how much to charge.
	• Data collection: ICD codes are used to collect and analyze health data, which is important for public health research and planning.
	• Who uses them: Healthcare providers, hospitals, and other healthcare organizations use ICD codes.
Insurance lobby:	Healthcare insurance lobbyists work to influence legislation, regulations, or government decisions on behalf of healthcare insurance companies, associations, or other related organizations. They aim to shape policies that benefit their clients, whether it's advocating for lower taxes, more favorable regulations, or influencing the direction of healthcare reform. They represent a wide range of interests within the healthcare insurance industry, including insurance companies,

	pharmaceutical companies, hospitals, and other healthcare providers.
	How they do it: Lobbyists engage in activities to influence policymakers
	<ul><li>Direct lobbying: Meeting with elected officials and their staff to present their arguments and persuade them to vote in a certain way.</li><li>Grassroots lobbying: Mobilizing public support for or against specific policies by encouraging constituents to contact their representatives.</li><li>Providing information: Offering research, data, and analysis to policymakers to support their arguments.</li><li>Building relationships: Establishing and maintaining strong relationships with policymakers and their staff to build trust and influence.</li></ul>
Insurance summary plan benefits (SPB):	These provide employees with a clear, understandable overview of their employer-sponsored benefits plans, including health insurance and retirement plans, in plain language. <ul><li>Purpose of an SPB: The SPB is designed to help employees understand the details of their benefits coverage, making it easier for them to navigate and utilize their plans.</li><li>What it covers: A SPB typically outlines the types of benefits offered, eligibility requirements, coverage details (e.g., deductibles, co-pays, maximums), and how to file claims.</li><li>Importance of SPB: It's a crucial tool for communication, ensuring they are informed about their benefits and can</li></ul>

	make informed decisions about their healthcare and retirement planning.
Lobbying expenditures:	Healthcare lobbying expenditures totaled $237 million in 2000. Healthcare lobbying expenditure accounted for 15% of all federal lobbying and was larger than the expenditures of every other sector.
Managed Medicare/Medicaid plans	Healthcare delivery systems organized to manage cost, utilization, and quality. Medicare and Medicaid managed care provide for the delivery of health benefits and additional services through contracted arrangements between state Medicaid agencies and managed care organizations (MCOs) that accept a set per-member-per-month (capitation) payment for these services. Many states use MCOs to deliver Medicare and Medicaid benefits, with a significant portion of Medicaid beneficiaries enrolled in comprehensive managed care organizations (MCOs). Benefits: • Cost control: MCOs can help control healthcare costs by negotiating lower rates with providers and managing utilization. • Improved quality: MCOs can improve quality by coordinating care, using evidence-based guidelines, and monitoring outcomes. Potential drawbacks: • Limited choice: MCOs can limit members' choice of providers and specialists. • Administrative complexity: MCOs can have complex rules and procedures that can be difficult for members to navigate. • Potential for bias: MCOs may be incentivized to deny or delay care to

	control costs, potentially impacting access to care for patients with chronic conditions or medical complexity.
Number of organizations involved:	In 2000, a total of 1192 organizations were involved in healthcare lobbying. From 1997 to 2000, the number of organizations increased by 50%.
Out-of-pocket cost:	This refers to the expenses patients pay directly from their own funds, without reimbursement from insurance or another source for medical services.
Prior authorization:	A health insurance company requires a doctor or specialist to submit medical details to obtain specific approval from them before providing certain medical treatments to patients. However, obtaining prior authorization is not a guarantee that the insurance plan will cover the cost of the medical treatment.
Premium:	A premium is the amount of money an individual or business pays regularly (usually monthly or annually) to an insurance company for coverage.
Utilization Management:[1]	Utilization management is a set of techniques used by providers of healthcare benefits to manage healthcare costs by influencing patient care decision-making through case-by-case assessments of care prior to its provision.

---

[1] Institute of Medicine (US) Committee on Utilization Management by Third Parties; Gray BH, Field MJ, editors. Controlling Costs and Changing Patient Care? The Role of Utilization Management. Washington (DC): National Academies Press (US); 1989. 1, Utilization Management: Introduction and Definitions. Available from: https://www.ncbi.nlm.nih.gov/books/NBK234995/

A Look at Systems of Healthcare

The United Nations and the World Health Organization (WHO) consider access to healthcare a fundamental human right.

Specifically, the WHO constitution states that "the enjoyment of the highest attainable standard of health is one of the fundamental rights of every human being." It goes on to say that countries have a legal obligation to develop and implement policies that guarantee universal access to quality health services and address the root causes of health disparities.

The concept of universal health coverage (UHC) is seen as a way to realize the right to health by ensuring that all people have affordable, equitable access to health services. However, when the general public considers healthcare as a "right", the immediate inspiration is what has been publicized in sound bites, left-leaning political rhetoric, or a comparison to the Canadian model of healthcare. Can we step back for a moment to consider how society benefits as a whole from a healthy populace? Nation-building, state-building, and public-private partnerships, all in some way, hinge on a healthy population. A nation's relative macroeconomic success, measured as GNP or GDP, also hinges on a healthy population. Health is humanity's greatest wealth.

The challenge societies have is not to focus solely on the cost of healthcare but on the benefits of healthy populations. "Spend a little today, save a ton tomorrow."

Low-cost preventative measures like free vaccination campaigns and mobile health clinics are programs that can reduce reliance on hospital-based care in developing and developed national contexts. We live in an age where we have an ever-increasing opportunity to leverage technology and artificial intelligence for early, health-related interventions. Through the deployment of mobile health platforms for rural populations, including education and telemedicine, technology can help address preventative and treatment-related efforts.

America's population is aging. In the US, elder care, Medicare, and Medicare costs will increase as the "boomer" population ages. Preventative care initiatives, like "healthier SG" in Singapore, that integrate social prescriptions addressing social determinants of health through low-cost methods, will reduce the overall economic impact of aging. Healthier elders mean fewer labor market adjustments. In Japan, the promotion of healthcare has seen its elderly citizens working later into life. This is a feasible goal of "healthcare as a right," enhancing workforce retention and productivity by promoting health and ensuring older adults remain engaged.

The Japanese have also exemplified how early investment in effective prevention reduced morbidity and functional disability from elderly chronic illnesses.

Why do we need healthcare, and why is it important? Most obviously, healthcare is essential for maintaining and improving individual health, enabling people to live longer, more fulfilling lives, and contributing longer to society. Healthcare allows individuals to work, learn, and enjoy their families and communities. It also has microeconomic benefits because it can lead to a healthier workforce, reduced healthcare costs in the long run, and a more productive local economy.

Comparing healthcare systems globally reveals diverse models with varying strengths and weaknesses. Some countries, like Canada, have universal single-payer systems, while others, like the US, have mixed public-private systems, and some, like Switzerland, have universal coverage through a heavily regulated private system.

- **Universal single-payer:**
  The government provides universal coverage, but healthcare is delivered by private providers, as in Canada.
- **Mixed public-private:**
  A combination of government and private insurance, like in the United States.
- **Universal coverage through private insurance:**
  A system where everyone is required to have private insurance, but with government regulation, as in Switzerland.
- **Bismarck model:**
  Healthcare is funded through a combination of employer and employee contributions, with private providers, as seen in Germany.
- **Beveridge model:**
  Healthcare is provided and funded by the government, with free access for all citizens, as in the UK.
- **Fee-for-service (out-of-pocket model):**
  Individuals pay for healthcare services directly, as in some developing countries.

Key considerations in comparing healthcare systems:

- **Coverage:**
  Universal coverage ensures that everyone has access to healthcare, while mixed systems may leave some uninsured.

- **Funding:**
  Public funding, like taxes, or private funding through insurance premiums, affects costs and accessibility.
- **Access to care:**
  Universal systems generally have better access, while private systems may have longer wait times or higher costs.
- **Cost:**
  The US spends significantly more on healthcare as a percentage of GDP than other developed countries, but health outcomes are not necessarily better.
- **Health outcomes:**
  While some systems may have better outcomes, others may have better access or lower costs.
- **Administrative efficiency:**
  Some systems are more efficient in terms of administration and reducing bureaucratic hurdles.
- **Equity:**
  Universal systems aim for equitable access to care, while private systems may lead to disparities based on income.

Examples of different systems in action:
- **Canada:**
  Has a universal, single-payer system funded through taxes, ensuring all residents have access to medically necessary hospital and physician services.
- **United States:**
  Has a mixed public-private system, with a significant portion of the population uninsured and high healthcare costs.

- **Germany:**
  Employs a Bismarck model, with private providers and funding through employer and employee contributions.
- **United Kingdom:**
  Has a Beveridge model, with a publicly funded National Health Service (NHS) providing free healthcare at the point of use.
- **Switzerland:**
  Has a universal, heavily regulated private system where private insurance is compulsory.

Numerous organizations have undertaken comparative studies in healthcare systems including the Commonwealth Fund, which conducts international health policy surveys and publishes reports comparing healthcare systems in various countries; the National Bureau of Economic Research (NBER) that studies the US and Canadian healthcare systems, and the Peterson-Kaiser Health System Tracker that tracks healthcare costs and utilization in the US and compares these data to other countries. Every study without exception finds that America spends far more on healthcare per capita, with generally worse outcomes, with the majority of the cost associated with acute inpatient and outpatient sick care.

In the *Intelligencer* article we have drawn from in this book, Wendell Potter says, "These companies are even bigger — far bigger — than they were when I was in the industry." "They use a lot of their money on campaign contributions, on lobbying, on propaganda campaigns to protect the status quo."[1]

---

[1] Dawsey, J., & Mathews, A. W. (2025, February 18). *Inside Trump's million-dollar dinners with healthcare executives. The Wall Street Journal.* Retrieved from https://www.wsj.com/politics/policy/trump-mar-o-lago-corporate-dinners-healthcare-executives-a8f171b0

Insurance companies are making sure their voices are heard.

It's time for us to make sure our voices are heard, too, louder and clearer than those of the insurers. There are many more of us than there are of them.

If you want to see change or you want to make a difference, here is a template you can use to write to your representative at the local, state, or national level. Letters and emails do have an impact.

Title   Date
Address
City, State, Zip Code

Dear Legislator,

I am a concerned voter who just read the book, *The Invisible Hand Wielding the Scalpel,* by Dr. Erica Rowe Urquhart.

The author detailed just how unfair our current government-backed healthcare plans are to patients like me, who are your constituents.

I am very concerned about the use of unfair prior authorization practices within managed Medicare and Medicaid plans. These utilization management practices are being used to delay or prevent patients like me from getting the care we so desperately need, including physical therapy, MRI, CT, surgical procedures, and oncology treatments. I am also concerned about the low reimbursements from Medicare and Medicaid that have contributed to the financial insolvency of local healthcare systems and medical practices.

Until federally backed healthcare reimbursements match the cost of care, supplies, implants, instrumentation, staffing, and ancillary services, our hospitals and doctors' offices will continue to be at risk for closure. Please consider proposing legislation to regulate prior authorization and utilization management practices. I am also relying on your office to investigate and propose legislation to increase the reimbursements from Medicare and Medicaid to the local healthcare providers I depend on for my health and well-being.

Sincerely,
Concerned taxpayer

About the Author

The intersection of healthcare and insurance is a battleground where medical providers are stressed by financial and administrative pressures. Dr. Erica Rowe Urquhart, a leading orthopedic surgeon in private practice, is sounding the alarm on how insurance companies' control over funding is fueling burnout among healthcare professionals, perpetuating inequities, and compromising patient care.

Before graduating from a magnet high school in San Diego, Dr. Urquhart was distinguished as "America's Top Student Leader" by the National Association of Secondary School Principals and was recognized as "Science Student of the Year" at the California State Science Fair. Dr. Urquhart left San Diego for Cambridge, Massachusetts, as a Harvard National Scholar. While at Harvard, she majored in biomedical engineering while completing her premedical requirements. Upon graduation from Harvard, Dr. Urquhart attended the Johns Hopkins University School of Medicine, where she completed her M.D. and obtained a Ph.D. in molecular and cellular neuroscience in seven years.

Dr. Erica Rowe Urquhart was selected for orthopedic surgery residency at the Cornell University-affiliated, all-orthopedic Hospital for Special Surgery. As a resident, she was recognized by the Orthopedic Research and Education Foundation for her developmental biology research performed at Cornell University.

After completing orthopedic surgery residency, Dr. Urquhart joined her husband, Marc, in private practice, and they formed Urquhart Orthopedic Associates in northern New Jersey. She has been a partner in the practice for two decades. In response to the myriad of insurance challenges her practice has faced, Dr. Urquhart obtained her mid-career Executive Master of Business Administration from The University of Oxford, Saïd Business School.

Dr. Rowe Urquhart lives with her husband, two children, and a dog.